HISTORY

Reflections of a Mormon Historian

HISTORY AND FAITH
Reflections of a Mormon Historian

Richard D. Poll

SIGNATURE BOOKS

SALT LAKE CITY

1989

for Gene

© 1989 by Signature Books, Inc. All rights reserved
Signature Books is a registered trademark of Signature Books, Inc.
Printed in the United States of America
96 95 94 93 92 91 90 89   6 5 4 3 2 1

Cover design: Easton Design
Interior design: Connie Disney

Library of Congress Cataloging-in-Publication Data

Poll, Richard Douglas, 1918–
  History and faith : reflections of a Mormon historian / Richard D.
Poll.
   p. cm.
  ISBN 0-941214-75-3
   1. Church of Jesus Christ of Latter-Day Saints — Historiography.
2. Mormon Church — Historiography. 3. Poll, Richard Douglas, 1918–
I. Title.
BX8611.P64 1989
289.3'09 — dc19   88-30198
                             CIP

COVER PHOTO: MRS. ALBERT MANWARING AND CHILDREN, SPRINGVILLE, UTAH, 1903;
BY GEORGE EDWARD ANDERSON, COURTESY OF RELL G. FRANCIS

Contents

Introduction

THE FOLLOWING ESSAYS ARE NOT TECHNICAL, SCHOLARLY PIECES, offering newly discovered information about Mormon history or doctrine. They are interpretative and reflective products of a lifetime of active membership in and studying and teaching about the Church of Jesus Christ of Latter-day Saints. The moral values they emphasize are tolerance, consistency, and commitment. The conviction they share — that the pursuit of knowledge, including historical knowledge, is virtuous (D&C 130:18-19; 131:6; 88:78-79, 118) — was best epitomized a half-century ago by a dear friend and mentor: "I believe that the gateway to heaven is strait and narrow; I also believe that it is high enough for me to take my head in with me."

The ten selections included here are all derived from public addresses. With the exception of the first, a sacrament meeting sermon, they were given in secular settings to predominantly Mormon audiences. In preparing them for publication, pertinent subsequent events have been taken into account and editorial changes have been made to give each present-day relevance. Several favorite ideas were used in more than one of the lectures, and it has not always been feasible to excise the repetitions. Nor has editing eliminated all stylistic evidence that these pieces were originally designed for a listening rather than a reading audience. The usual textual observations about bibliography have generally been deleted, and no attempt has been made to provide full documentation. The authors to whom I am primarily indebted are acknowledged at appropriate places.

Three of the essays that follow have been previously published, sometimes in a slightly different form. "What the Church Means to People Like Me," a talk given in the Palo Alto Ward in August 1967, first appeared in *Dialogue: A Journal of Mormon Thought* 2 (Winter 1967): 107-17. Because of the apparent usefulness of the Liahona-Iron

Rod symbolism it introduced, it was subsequently printed in the RLDS *Saints' Herald* 115 (15 Oct. 1968): 15-16; *Sunstone* 5 (July-Aug. 1980): 15-20; in Philip L. Barlow, ed., *A Thoughtful Faith* (Centerville, UT: Canon Press, 1986), 1-15; and in Mary L. Bradford, ed., *Personal Voices: A Celebration of Dialogue* (Salt Lake City: Signature Books, 1987), 49-62.

"Liahona and Iron Rod Revisited" was presented at the September 1982 meeting of the John Whitmer Historical Association in Independence, Missouri, and was published in *Dialogue: A Journal of Mormon Thought* 16 (Summer 1983): 69-78.

"God and Man in History," my presidential address to the Mormon History Association annual meeting in Los Angeles in April 1970, appeared in *Dialogue: A Journal of Mormon Thought* 7 (Spring 1972): 101-109.

None of the other seven addresses has been published in its entirety before, although major elements were incorporated in presentations to Sunstone symposiums in Salt Lake City and Washington, D.C., and appeared in "The Swearing Elders: Some Reflections," *Sunstone* 10 (1986), 9: 14-17; and in "Dealing With Dissonance: Myths, Documents and Faith," *Sunstone* 12 (May 1988): 17-21.

"The Happy Valley Syndrome" was given at Brigham Young University, 19 November 1969, as part of the "Mormonism Meets the Issues" series, sponsored by the Academics Office of the Associated Students of BYU. It had some special interest for both speaker and audience because I would soon be leaving BYU, having accepted appointment as Vice-President for Administration at Western Illinois University.

"Of Ignorance and Action" was delivered at the Brigham Young University College of Social Sciences convocation, 21 August 1969. The selection of the topic was prompted by the anti-war and anti-Communist movements then rampant.

The next four essays are derived from a series of six lectures presented under the title, "Our Changing Past: Reflections of a Mormon Historian," at Brigham Young University in October and November 1984. The series was sponsored by the Faculty Academy, a joint enterprise of the colleges of biological and agricultural sciences, family and social sciences, and physical and mathematical sciences. In the order of their presentation, the original titles were: "Our History: Myths and Documents"; "Our Church: Continuity and Change"; "Our Heroes: Thomas L. Kane as Case Study"; "Our Secrets: Confronting the Skeletons"; "Our State: Utah and the Mormons"; and "Our Prophets: God's Human Spokesmen."

The third and fifth of these lectures have been previously published as *Quixotic Mediator: Thomas L. Kane and the Utah War* (Ogden, UT: Weber State College, 1985) and "Utah and the Mormons: A Symbiotic Relationship," in Davis Bitton and Maureen Ursenbach Beecher, eds., *New Views of Mormon History: Essays in Honor of Leonard J. Arrington* (Salt Lake City: University of Utah Press, 1987), 323-41. They are not included in this collection because they are more representative of the historian's craft than of the implications and problems of studying and writing Mormon history.

Elements from the first and sixth lectures, the conclusions from all six, and material from other personal essays and addresses are incorporated in the final essay of this collection, "The Challenge of Living With Change," which was written specially for this volume.

I am grateful to all who reacted to the addresses when they were given, including the critics who moved me to reexamine both my facts and my faith. I acknowledge particularly the thoughtful suggestions of my brother Carl, with whom I have enjoyed an ongoing dialogue although we have lived miles apart since I first came to Brigham Young University in 1948. My daughters and sons-in-law have patiently listened and perceptively probed, and my wife, Gene, has been a source of strength since we met under a Miami moon forty-five years ago.

Thanks also to Signature Books for offering these essays to a wider audience and for making helpful editorial suggestions. The final responsibility for what follows is, of course, mine. The factual information is believed to be accurate; the interpretations, evaluations, and conclusions are for the reader to judge. I hope that those who choose to delve and ponder will be entertained, informed, perplexed, amused, bemused, stimulated, disillusioned, excited, aggravated, motivated, and inspired by what they find here.

I

What the Church Means
to People Like Me

A NATURAL REACTION TO MY TITLE MIGHT BE, "WHO CARES?"
For who, with the possible exception of my brother, Carl, are "people
like me"? I have a wife and daughters who find me in some respects
unique. I am sure there were students at Brigham Young University
and Western Illinois University who *hoped* that I was unique. And by
the time I have finished there may be some among my readers who
will share that hope.

Yet I have chosen the topic because I believe that in some
important respects I represent a type of Latter-day Saint found in
almost every ward and branch in the church. By characterizing myself
and explaining the nature of my commitment to the gospel of the
Church of Jesus Christ of Latter-day Saints, I hope to contribute a
little something of value to each of you, whether it turns out that you
are "people like me" or not.

My thesis is that there are two types of active and dedicated
Latter-day Saints. I am not talking about "good Mormons" and "Jack
Mormons," or about Saints in white hats and pseudo-Saints in black.
No, I am talking about two types of *involved* church members, each
deeply committed to the gospel but also prone toward misgivings
about the legitimacy, adequacy, or serviceability of the commitment
of the other.

The purpose of my inquiry is not to support either set of
misgivings but to describe each type as dispassionately as I can, to
identify myself with one of the types, and then to bear witness

I

concerning some of the blessings which the Mormon church offers to the type I identify with. My hope is that this effort will help us all to look beyond the things which obviously differentiate us toward that "unity of the faith" which Jesus Christ set as our common goal.

For convenience of reference, let me propose symbols for my two types of Mormons. They have necessarily to be affirmative images, because I am talking only about "good" members. I found them in the Book of Mormon, a natural place for a Latter-day Saint to find good symbols as well as good counsel.

The figure for the first type comes from Lehi's dream—the Iron Rod. The figure for the second comes also from Lehi's experience—the Liahona. So similar they are as manifestations of God's concern for his children, yet just different enough to suit my purposes.

The Iron Rod, as the hymn reminds us, was the word of God. To the person with a hand on the rod, each step of the journey to the tree of life was plainly defined; one had only to hold on while moving forward. In Lehi's dream the way was *not easy*, but it was *clear*.

The Liahona, in contrast, was a compass. It pointed to the destination but did not fully mark the path; indeed, the clarity of its directions varied with the circumstances of the user. For the members of Lehi's family the sacred instrument was a reminder of their temporal and eternal goals, but it was not an infallible delineator of their course.

Even as the Iron Rod and the Liahona were both approaches to the word and kingdom of God, so our two types of church members seek the word and the kingdom. The fundamental difference between them lies in their concept of the relation of men and women to the "word of God." Put another way, it is a difference in the meaning assigned to the concept "the fullness of the gospel." Do the revelations of our Heavenly Father give us a handrail to the kingdom or a compass only?

The Iron Rod Saint does not look for questions but for answers and in the gospel—as he or she understands it—finds or is confident that the answer to every important question can be found. The Liahona Saint, on the other hand, is preoccupied with questions and skeptical of answers, finding in the gospel—as he or she understands it—answers to enough important questions so as to function purposefully without answers to the rest. This last sentence holds the key to the question posed by my title, but before pursuing its implications let us explore this scheme of classification more fully.

As I suggested at the outset, I find Iron Rods and Liahonas in almost every LDS congregation, discernible by the kinds of comments they make in gospel doctrine classes and the language in which they phrase their testimonies. What gives them their original bent is difficult to identify. The Iron Rods may be somewhat more common among converts, but many nowadays are attracted to the Mormon church by reasons more appropriate to Liahonas. Liahona testimonies may be more prevalent among lifelong members who have not had an emotional conversion experience, but many such have developed Iron Rod commitments in the home, the Sunday school, the mission field, or some other conditioning environment. Social and economic status appear to have nothing to do with type, and the rather widely held notion that education tends to produce Liahonas has so many exceptions that one may plausibly argue that education only makes Liahonas more articulate. Parenthetically, some of the most prominent Iron Rods in the church are on the BYU faculty.

Pre-existence may, I suppose, have something to do with placement in this classification, even as it may account for other life circumstances, but heredity obviously does not. The irritation of the Iron Rod father confronted by an iconoclastic son or daughter is about as commonplace as the embarrassment of the Liahona parent who discovers that her teenager has found comfortable answers in seminary to some of the questions that have perplexed her all her life.

The picture is complicated by the fact that changes of type do occur, often in response to profoundly unsettling personal experiences. The Liahona member who, in a context of despair or repentance, makes the "leap of faith" to Iron Rod commitment is rare, I think, but the investigator of Liahona temperament who becomes an Iron Rod convert is almost typical. The Iron Rod member who responds to personal tragedy or intellectual shock by becoming a Liahona is known to us all; this transition may be but is not necessarily a stage in a migration toward inactivity or even apostasy. My opinion is that one's identification with the Iron Rods or the Liahonas is more a function of basic temperament and of accidents than of premortal accomplishments or mortal choices, but that opinion — like many other views expressed in this essay — has neither scriptural nor scientific validation.

A point to underscore in terms of our objective of "unity of faith" is that Iron Rods and Liahonas have great difficulty understanding each other — not at the level of intellectual acceptance of the right to peaceful co-existence but at the level of personal communion, of empathy. To the Iron Rod a questioning attitude suggests an imperfect faith; to the Liahona an unquestioning spirit betokens a closed mind. Neither frequent association nor even prior personal involvement with the other group guarantees empathy. Indeed, the person who has crossed the line is likely to be least sympathetic and tolerant toward his erstwhile kindred spirits.

I have suggested that the essential difference between the Liahonas and the Iron Rods is in their approach to the concept "the word of God." Let us investigate that now a little.

The Iron Rod is confident that, on any question, the mind and will of the Lord may be obtained. His sources are threefold: scripture, prophetic authority, and the Holy Spirit. In the standard works of the church the Iron Rod member finds more answers than does his Liahona brother, because he accepts them as God's word in a far more literal sense. In them he finds answers to questions as diverse as the age and origin of the earth, the justification for capital punishment, the proper diet, the proper role of government, the nature and functions of sex, and the nature of man. To the Liahona, he sometimes seems to be reading things into the printed words, but to himself the meaning is clear.

In the pronouncements of the General Authorities, living and dead, the Iron Rod finds many answers, because he accepts and gives comprehensive application to that language of the Doctrine and Covenants which declares: "And whatsoever they shall speak when moved upon by the Holy Ghost shall be scripture, shall be the will of the Lord, shall be the mind of the Lord, and the power of God unto salvation" (68:4). This reliance extends to every facet of life. On birth control and family planning, labor relations and civil liberties, the meaning of the Constitution and prospects for the United Nations, the laws of health and the signs of the times, the counsel of the "living oracles" suffices. Where answers are not found in the published record, they are sought in correspondence and interviews, and once received, they are accepted as definitive.

Third among the sources for the Iron Rod member is the Holy Spirit. As Joseph Smith found answers in the counsel of James, "If any of you lack wisdom, let him ask of God," so any Latter-day Saint may do so. Whether it be the choice of a vocation or the choice of a mate, help on a college examination or in finding "Golden Prospects" in the mission field, healing the sick or averting a divorce — in prayer is the answer. The response may not be what was expected, but it *will* come, and it will be a manifestation of the Holy Spirit.

Implicit in all this is the confidence of the Iron Rod Latter-day Saint that our Heavenly Father is intimately involved in the day-to-day business of his children. As no sparrow falls without the Father, so nothing befalls men or women without his will. God knows the answers to all questions and has the solutions to all problems, and the only thing which denies people access to this reservoir is their own stubbornness. Truly then men and women who open their mind and heart to the channels of revelation, past and present, have the Iron Rod which leads unerringly to the kingdom.

The Liahona Latter-day Saint lacks this certain confidence. Not that he or she rejects the concepts upon which it rests — that God lives, that he loves his children, that his knowledge and power are efficacious for salvation, and that he does reveal his will as the Ninth Article of Faith affirms. Nor does he reserve the right of selective obedience to the will of God as he understands it. No, the problem for the Liahona involves the adequacy of the *sources* on which the Iron Rod testimony depends.

The problem is in perceiving the will of God when it is mediated — as it is for almost all mortals — by "the arm of flesh." The Liahona is convinced by logic and experience that no human instrument, even a prophet, is capable of transmitting the word of God so clearly and comprehensively that it can be universally understood and easily appropriated by all humanity.

Because the Liahona finds it impossible to accept the literal verbal inspiration of the standard works, the sufficiency of scriptural answers to questions automatically comes into question. If Eve was not made from Adam's rib, how much of the Bible is historic truth? If geology and anthropology have undermined Bishop Ussher's chronology, which places creation at about 4,000 B.C., how much of the Bible is scientific truth? And if latter-day scriptures have been significantly revised since their original publication, can it be assumed that they are now infallibly authoritative? To the Liahona these volumes are sources of inspiration and moral truth, but they leave many specific questions unanswered, or uncertainly answered.

As for the authority of the Latter-day prophets, the Liahona Saint finds consensus among them on gospel fundamentals but far-ranging diversity on many important issues. The record shows error, as in Brigham Young's statements about the continuation of slavery, and it shows change of counsel, as in the matter of gathering to Zion. It shows differences of opinion—Heber J. Grant and Reed Smoot on the League of Nations, and David O. McKay and Joseph Fielding Smith on the process of creation. To the Liahonas, the "living oracles" are God's special witnesses of the gospel of Jesus Christ and his agents in directing the affairs of the church, but like the scriptures, they leave many important questions unanswered, or uncertainly answered.

The Iron Rod proposition that the Holy Spirit will supply what the prophets have not gives difficulty on both philosophical and experimental grounds. Claims that prayer is an infallible, almost contractual, link between God and man through the Holy Spirit find Liahona Mormons perplexed by the nature of the evidence. As a method of confirming truth, the witness of the Spirit demonstrably has *not* produced uniformity of gospel interpretation even among Iron Rod Saints, and it is allegedly by the witness of that same Spirit—by the burning within—that many apostates pronounce the whole church in error. As a method of influencing the course of events, it seems unpredictable and some of the miracles claimed for it seem almost whimsical. By the prayer of faith, one person recovers lost eyeglasses; in spite of such prayer, another goes blind.

All of which leaves the Liahona Mormon with a somewhat tenuous connection with the Holy Spirit. He may take comfort in his imperfect knowledge from that portion of the Article of Faith which says that "God will yet reveal many great and important things." And he may reconcile his conviction of God's love and his observation of the uncertain earthly outcomes of faith by emphasizing the divine commitment to the principle of free agency. In any case, it seems to the Liahona Mormon that God's involvement in day-to-day affairs must be less active and intimate than the Iron Rod Mormon believes, because there are so many unsolved problems and unanswered prayers.

Is the Iron Rod member unaware of these considerations which loom so large in the Liahona member's relationship to the word of

God? In some instances, I believe, the answer is yes. For in our activity-centered church, it is quite possible to be deeply and satisfyingly involved without looking seriously at the philosophical implications of some gospel propositions which are professed.

In many instances, however, the Iron Rod Saint has found sufficient answers to the Liahona questions. He sees so much basic consistency in the scriptures and the teachings of the latter-day prophets that the apparent errors and incongruities can be handled by interpretation. He finds so much evidence of the immanence of God in human affairs that the apparently pointless evil and injustice in the world can be handled by the valid assertion that God's ways are not man's ways. He is likely to credit his Liahona contemporaries with becoming so preoccupied with certain problems that they cannot see the gospel forest for the trees, and he may even attribute that preoccupation to an insufficiency of faith. As a Liahona, I must resist the attribution, although I cannot deny the preoccupation.

Both kinds of Mormons have problems — not just the ordinary personal problems to which all flesh is heir, but problems growing out of the nature of their church commitment. The Iron Rod has a natural tendency to develop answers where none may, in fact, have been revealed. He may find arguments against Social Security in the Book of Mormon; he may discover in esoteric prophetic utterances a timetable for that Second Coming of which "that day and hour knoweth no man." His dogmatism may become offensive to his peers in the church and a barrier to communication with his own family; his confidence in his own insights may make him impatient with those whom he publicly sustains. He may also cling to cherished answers in the face of new revelation or be so shaken by innovation that he forms new "fundamentalist" sects. The Iron Rod concept holds many firm in the church, but it can also lead some out.

The Liahona, on the other hand, has the temptation to broaden the scope of questioning until even the most clearly defined church doctrines and policies are included. His resistance to statistics on principle may deteriorate into a carping criticism of programs and leaders. His ties to the church may become so nebulous that he cannot communicate them to his children. His testimony may become so selective as to exclude him from some forms of church activity or to make him a hypocrite in his own eyes as he participates in them. His persistence in doubting may alienate his brethren and eventually destroy the substance of his gospel commitment. Then he too is out — without fireworks but not without pain.

Both kinds of Latter-day Saints serve the church. They talk differently and apparently think and feel differently about the gospel, but as long as they avoid the extremes just mentioned, they share a love for and commitment to the church. They cannot therefore be distinguished on the basis of attendance at meetings, participation on welfare projects, contributions, or faithfulness in the performance of callings. They may or may not be one hundred percenters, but the degree of their activity is not a function of type, insofar as I have been able to observe. (It may be that Iron Rods are a little more faithful in genealogical work, but even this is not certain.)

Both kinds of members are found at every level of church responsibility — in bishoprics and Relief Society presidencies, in stake presidencies and high councils, and even among the General Authorities. But whatever their private orientation, the public deportment of the General Authorities seems to me to represent a compromise, which would be natural in the circumstances. They satisfy the Iron Rods by emphasizing the solid core of revealed truth and by discouraging speculative inquiry into matters of faith and morals, and they comfort the Liahonas by resisting the pressure to make pronouncements on all subjects and by reminding the Saints that God has not revealed the answer to every question or defined the response to every prayer.

As I have suggested, the Iron Rods and the Liahonas have some difficulty understanding each other. Lacking the patience, wisdom, breadth of experience, or depth of institutional commitment of the General Authorities, we sometimes criticize and judge each other. But usually we live and let live — each finding in the church what meets one's own needs and all sharing the gospel blessings which do not depend on identity of testimony.

Which brings me to the second part of my essay — the part which gives it its title: What the Church Means to People Like Me.

Although I have tried to characterize two types of Latter-day Saints with objectivity, I can speak with conviction only about one example from one group. In suggesting — briefly — what the church offers to a Liahona like me, I hope to provoke all of us to reexamine the nature of our own commitments and to grow in understanding and love for those whose testimonies are defined in different terms.

By my initial characterization of types, I am the kind of Mormon who is preoccupied with questions and skeptical of answers. I find in the gospel — as I understand it — answers to enough important questions so that I can function purposefully, and I hope effectively, without present answers to the rest.

The primary question of this generation, it seems to me, is the question of meaning. Does life really add up to anything at all? At least at the popular level, the philosophy of existentialism asks, and tries to answer, the question of how to function significantly in a world which apparently has no meaning. When the philosophy is given a religious context, it becomes an effort to salvage some of the values of traditional religion for support in this meaningless world.

To the extent that existence is seen as meaningless — even absurd — human experiences have only immediate significance. A drug-induced hallucinogenic experience stands on a par with a visit to the Sistine Chapel or a concert of the Tabernacle Choir. What the individual does with himself — or other "freely consenting adults" — is nobody's business, regardless of what it involves.

For me, the gospel answers this question of meaning, and the answer is grandly challenging. It lies in three revealed propositions: (1) man — that is, men and women — is eternal, (2) man is free, and (3) God's work and glory is to exalt this eternal free agent — man.

The central conception is freedom. With a belief in the doctrine of free agency, I can cope with some of the riddles and tragedies which are cited in support of the philosophy of the absurd. In the nature of human freedom — as I understand it — is to be found the reconciliation of the concept of a loving God and the facts of an unlovely world.

The restored gospel teaches that the essential stuff of humankind is eternal, that we are all children of God, and that it is our destiny to become like our heavenly parents. But this destiny can only be achieved as we *voluntarily* gain the knowledge, the experience, and the discipline which godhood requires and represents. *This* was the crucial question resolved in the council in heaven — whether we should come into an environment of genuine risk, where we would walk by faith.

To me, this prerequisite for exaltation explains the apparent remoteness of God from many aspects of the human predicament — my predicament. My range of freedom is left large, and arbitrary divine interference with that freedom is kept minimal in order that I may grow. Were God's hand always upon my shoulder or an Iron Rod always in my grasp, my range of free choice would be constricted and my growth as well.

This view does not rule out miraculous interventions by our Heavenly Father, but it does not permit their being commonplace. What is seen as miracle by the Iron Rod Saints, my type tends to interpret as coincidence or psychosomatic manifestation or inaccurately remembered or reported event. The same attitude is even more likely with regard to the Satanic role in human affairs. The conflict between good and evil—with its happy and unhappy outcomes—is seen more often as a derivative of human nature and environment than as a contest between titanic powers for the capture of human pawns. If God cannot, in the ultimate sense, coerce the eternal intelligences which are embodied in his children, then how much less is Lucifer able to do so. We may yield to the promptings of good or evil, but we are *not* puppets.

There is another aspect of the matter. If, with or without prayer, we are arbitrarily spared the consequences of our own fallibility and the natural consequences of the kind of hazardous world in which we live, then freedom becomes meaningless and God capricious. If the law that fire burns, that bullets kill, that age deteriorates, and that the rain falls on the just and the unjust is sporadically suspended upon petition of faith, what happens to that reliable connection between cause and consequence which is a condition of knowledge. And what a peril to faith lies in the idea that God *can* break the causal chain, that he frequently *does* break it, but that in *my* individual case he may not *choose* to do so. This is the dilemma of theodicy, reconciling God's omnipotence with evil and suffering, which is so dramatically phrased: "If God is good, he is not God; if God is God, he is not good."

From what has been said, it must be apparent that Liahonas like me do not see prayer as a form of spiritual mechanics, in spite of such scriptural language as "Prove me herewith" and "I, the Lord, am bound." Prayer is rarely for miracles, or even for new answers. It is— or ought to be—an intensely personal exercise in sorting out and weighing the relevant factors in our problems and looking to God as we consider the alternative solutions. (Many of our problems would solve themselves if we would consider only options on which we could honestly ask God's benediction.) We might pray for a miracle, especially in time of deep personal frustration or tragedy, but we would think it presumptuous to command God and would not suspend the future on the outcome of the petition.

This is not to say that Liahonas cannot verbalize prayer as proficiently as their Iron Rod contemporaries. One cannot be significantly involved in the church without mastering the conventional prayer forms and learning to fit the petition to the proportions of the occasion. But even in public prayers it is possible, I believe, for the attentive ear to detect those differences which I have tried to describe. To oppose evil as we can, to bear adversity as we must, and to do our jobs well—these are the petitions in Liahona prayers. They invoke God's blessings, but they require our answering.

To this Liahona Latter-day Saint, God is powerful to save. He is pledged to keep the way of salvation open to me and to do, through the example and sacrifice of his son and the ordinances and teachings of his church, what I cannot do for myself. But beyond this, he has left things pretty much up to me—a free agent, a god in embryo who must learn by experience as well as direction how to be like God.

In this circumstance the Church of Jesus Christ performs three special functions for me. Without them, my freedom might well become unbearable.

In the first place, the church reminds me—almost incessantly—that what I do makes a difference. It matters to my fellow men and women because most of what I do or fail to do affects their progress toward salvation. And it matters to me, even if it has no discernible influence upon others. Even though life is eternal, time is short and I have none to waste.

In the second place, the church suggests and sometimes prescribes guidelines for the use of freedom. The deportment standards of the Ten Commandments and the Sermon on the Mount, the rules for mental and physical well-being in the Doctrine and Covenants, the reminders and challenges in the temple ceremony—these are examples, and they harmonize with free agency because even those which are prescribed are not coerced.

There is a difference here, I think, between the way Iron Rods and Liahonas look at the guidelines. Answer-oriented, the Iron Rods tend to spell things out; sabbath observance becomes no TV or movies, or TV but no movies, or uplifting TV and no other, or no studying, or studying for religion classes but no others. For Liahonas like me, the sabbath commandment is a reminder of the kinship of free men and a concerned and loving Father. What is fitting, not what is conventional, becomes the question. On a lovely autumn evening I may even, with quiet conscience, pass up a church fireside for a drive in the canyon. But the thankfulness for guidelines is nonetheless strong.

In the final place comes the contribution of the church in giving me something to relate to — to belong to — to *feel* a part of.

Contemporary psychology has much to say about the awful predicament of alienation. "The Lonely Crowd" is the way one expert describes it. Former Mormons often feel it; a good friend who somehow migrated out of the church put it this way: "I don't belong anywhere."

For the active Latter-day Saint such alienation is impossible. The church is an association of kindred spirits, a sub-culture, a "folk" — and this is the tie which binds Iron Rods and Liahonas together as strongly as the shared testimony of Joseph Smith. It is as fundamental to the solidarity of LDS families — almost — as the doctrine of eternal marriage itself. It makes brothers and sisters of the convert and the Daughter of the Utah Pioneers, of the Hong Kong branch president and the missionary from Cedar City. It unites congregations — the genealogists and the procrastinators, the old-fashioned patriarchs and the family planners, the eggheads and the doubters of "the wisdom of men."

This sense of belonging is what makes me feel at home in my ward. Liahonas and Iron Rods together, we are products of a great historic experience, laborers in a great enterprise, and sharers of a commitment to the proposition that life is important because God is real and we are his children — free agents with the opportunity to become heirs of his kingdom.

This is the witness of the Spirit to this Liahona Latter-day Saint. When the returning missionary warms her homecoming with a narrative of a remarkable conversion, I may note the inconsistency or naivete of some of her analysis, but I am moved nevertheless by the picture of lives transformed — made meaningful — by the gospel. When the home teachers call, I am sometimes self-conscious about the "role playing" in which we all seem to be engaged. Yet I ask my wife often — in our times of deepest concern and warmest parental satisfaction — what might our daughters have become without the church. When a dear friend passes, an accident victim, I may recoil from the well-meant suggestion that God's need for him was greater than his family's, but my lamentation is sweetened by the realization of what the temporal support of the Saints and the eternal promises of the Lord mean to those who mourn.

For this testimony, for the church which inspires and feeds it, and for fellowship in the church with the Iron Rods and Liahonas who share it, this Liahona thanks his Heavenly Father.

2

Liahona and
Iron Rod Revisited

Since the 1967 appearance of "What the Church Means to People Like Me," the Liahona-Iron Rod symbolism has taken on a life of its own. In addition to republications in periodicals and anthologies, hundreds of reprints and copies of the article have found their way into circulation, many through Brigham Young University's bookstore and classes and the LDS institute and seminary system. It was quoted in Gottlieb's and Wiley's *America's Saints* and figures prominently in the conclusion of Arrington's and Bitton's *The Mormon Experience*.[1] Its most significant contribution — to the extent that it went beyond providing handy labels — was to help make the Liahonas more accepting of themselves. As one correspondent succinctly put it to me: "You'll never know how delighted I was to find out that I have a nice name like Liahona. . . . I just wasn't aware that there were so many of us who questioned."

That was more than two decades ago. What has happened to Liahonas and Iron Rods in the years since LDS leader David O. McKay, RLDS leader W. Wallace Smith, and national leader Lyndon B. Johnson were all presidents in the land of Zion?

Like the 1967 sermon, what follows is a personal essay. It has no research base other than twenty more years of living as a Mormon and the observations of several friends on the two questions I propose to consider here.

The first question is: How has the concept of two basic types

15

of committed Latter-day Saints stood up under scrutiny and reflection?

Reactions to the Liahona-Iron Rod dichotomy — then and now — fall into three groups. Some accept what they interpret to be the classification scheme, identify themselves as Liahonas, and find comfort and encouragement therein. One friend recently wrote: "I personally think your talk helped reassure Liahonas that they could remain in the church in good conscience; many of them are now in leading positions in the church." A former member of one of the church's general boards wrote from the mission field in 1968: "I can't help being a Liahona, and it is important not to feel guilty about it. It is also important to accept the Iron Rods as they are." A BYU colleague expressed the hope that "some 'Iron Rods' may read this and through it better understand the questioning mind."

A second group is those who identify themselves as Iron Rods and have no intention of changing. However, their attitudes toward Liahonas are mixed. One stake president invited me to discuss the subject over dinner and accepted my assurances that the sermon was not intended to divide the Saints or to provoke questions among the unquestioning or to pass judgment on anyone. Others of the answer-oriented tendency were more critical — none more publicly than a counselor in the church's First Presidency. In a 1971 General Conference address entitled "The Iron Rod," he warned against those who "profess to be religious and speak of themselves as Christians, and according to one such 'as accepting the scriptures only as sources of inspiration and moral truth,' and then ask in smugness: 'Do the revelations of God give us a handrail to the kingdom of God, as the Lord's messenger told Lehi, or merely a compass?' "[2]

The third group of responses came — and still comes — from people who object to being pigeonholed. Their perspective was well expressed by a recent respondent to my request for advice: "Is there not a continuum along which individuals may be categorized in terms of their interpretation and application of the gospel rather than being placed in a discrete category?"

Considerable discussion and reflection have brought me to these qualifying and hopefully clarifying observations:

1. In the metaphoric sense which I have proposed, the Iron-Rod-Liahona dichotomy has elements in common with, but not synonymous with, such classifications as dogmatism and empiricism,

orthodoxy and heterodoxy, fundamentalism and modernism, or even conservatism and liberalism. However, the identification is far from complete. Iron Rod Saints have demonstrated remarkable flexibility in the matter of theology: they happily see blacks in the temple and stay home from church on Sunday evenings. Correspondingly, some Liahonas have defended evolution and the Equal Rights Amendment with fervent dogmatism. The labels of Liahona and Iron Rod identify responses to religious authoritarianism in the sphere of Latter-day Saint testimony, not predictable positions on given issues, certain attitudes, or any particular behavior patterns.

2. The classification is not a separation of the good guys from the bad guys. Virtue and unrighteousness are found in individuals of both types. I freely acknowledge a special sensibility to Iron Rod sins and sinners, but I am well aware of some perils that particularly beset the Liahona path. One is a tendency to swing from self-doubt clear through self-acceptance to self-congratulation. In the words of one of my recent correspondents: "Liahonas see themselves as somehow *outside* the pale; over there are all the plodders, the Iron Rodders, clinging blindly to pull themselves through the fog, while over here are we liahonas, basking in the light of superior knowledge." Another peril is poignantly described in a *Dialogue* article called "Some Sentimental Thoughts on Leaving the Fold." For its author the Liahona concept was a halfway house to existential atheism. Others like him have followed their doubts to some destination outside the fold, usually without fireworks but not without pain.[3]

3. The Liahona-Iron Rod symbolism relates more directly to the quest for truth than to the pursuit of virtue. It is useful to recall that Joseph Smith defined truth in terms of knowledge, declared it to be very important, and suggested that its pursuit would extend far beyond this life (see D&C 50:40; 84:19; 88:78–79; 93:23–36; 130:19). Thus, even the most knowledgeable Mormon lives with unanswered questions, with partial and tentative answers, and with authority-based answers that may not be persuasive to others. We should ask — Iron Rods and Liahonas alike — before entering into warm debate on any knowledge-related question: Is finding a "true" answer important to the business of Christ-like living? If we note how often our response turns out to be negative, we may be more content to let our brothers and sisters treasure their tentativeness or cherish their certitude, as the case might be.

4. The distinction between Liahona and Iron Rod is most clearly discernible in responses to the question: Is the more reliable test of the validity of a statement its substance or its source? It involves differing perspectives on the dual approach to knowledge propounded by Joseph Smith: "Seek learning, even by study and also by faith" (D&C 88:14). The Liahona is a "by study" person; he or she relies on the tests of "prove all things" and "by their fruits" because he or she regards no human authority as infallible. The Iron Rod sees some human authorities — prophets, scriptures, and inner promptings — as sufficiently reliable to be accepted "by faith." (Happily, the institutional church accepts wide latitude of belief among its members. It emphasizes obedience, but it excommunicates for apostasy only those who challenge its authority in a public and hostile manner.)

5. The potential to be Iron Rod or Liahona is in everyone, but it is possible to be an active Mormon without making a conscious intellectual choice to be either. This is so because a typical LDS commitment is not to a set of rigorously examined "truth" propositions but to a collection of activities, values, attitudes, hopes, customs, emotions, support systems, and verbal and visual symbols. The gospel, the church, the scriptures, and the prophets are "true" in that they are seen as the sources of these personalized components of a Latter-day Saint life. Nonconforming behavior need not undermine confidence in the "truth" of these sources as long as such behavior can be self-excused by some form of the "I'm only human" rationalization. An active Mormon may, in other words, act and talk like an Iron Rod because he has never actually confronted a serious question which has tested his confidence in the validity of religious authority. One of my favorite church leaders frequently quoted Will Durant: "No one deserves to believe unless he has served an apprenticeship of doubt."[4] It may be that the terms Liahona and Iron Rod should be applied only to those Mormons who have experienced that apprenticeship.

6. It may be that the most important single factor influencing whether one becomes an Iron Rod or a Liahona is vocational choice. Some occupations raise more questions and present more problems which seriously challenge religious authority than others. Education and emotional trauma also affect the outcome. As a consequence, among individual Latter-day Saints — converts as well as those reared in the church — there is more movement from Iron Rod to Liahona

than the reverse. Whether this is seen as a favorable or unfavorable trend, it is hardly surprising.

7. Certain characteristics of organizational behavior affect the way individuals of either persuasion function in the church. The impression among most of the laity — much stronger in the LDS than in the RLDS church — that the General Authorities agree on all matters of doctrine and policy gives disproportionate influence to idiosyncratic views which are publicly and dogmatically expressed by individuals in the church hierarchy. The institutional emphasis on compliance generates a certain bias toward placing Iron Rods in presiding positions at all levels of the organization, while calling Liahonas, as one of my correspondents wryly noted, "to teach classes, be Boy Scout leaders, and do all kinds of things that require goodness and sensitivity, but not so much unquestioning obedience." The primary criterion in the appointment process, however, is who — among the men and women available for prayerful consideration — is seen as most likely to get the job done. The consequence is a mixture of Liahonas and Iron Rods in offices and callings down to the ward level, and each member of the church finds that his or her operating environment is affected considerably by whether his or her immediate file leaders happen to be one or the other. Finally, the desire for acceptance in a conformity-stressing church leads to a certain amount of role playing to conceal both doubt and disobedience.[5] This blurs the distinction between Iron Rods and Liahonas and makes it easier for them to work together.

8. In the realm of both ideas and actions, Iron Rods and Liahonas can be quite utilitarian. Gospel "truth" may be eternal, but applications change in response to institutional and individual needs. Joseph Smith provided a rationale: "That which is wrong under one circumstance may be, and often is, right in another. . . . This is the principle on which the government of heaven is conducted — by revelation adapted to the circumstances in which the children of the kingdom are placed."[6] Of the adaptiveness of the institutional kingdom something will be said later. How the children of the kingdom also reshape gospel questions and answers to the circumstances of their own lives is beautifully expressed in the following excerpt from a letter: "Each Saint, will he or nil he, lives in a private world of doctrine, shaped to a great degree by Joseph Smith and his reinterpreters, but shaped much more profoundly by his own experience and his own

will, which have edited all doctrines and teachings into a private reality in which he dwells."

Having said all this, I reaffirm my impression that at any point in time an active Latter-day Saint can be identified as a Liahona or an Iron Rod by his or her initial response to questions and answers which bear seriously on his or her understanding of the gospel. Those who need "true" answers and see religious authority as a reliable source of such answers are Iron Rods. Those who see truth as elusive and *all* authority-based answers as liable to scrutiny are Liahonas. The Iron Rods pray for confirmation of answers which they have received, and frequently it comes. The Liahonas pray for strength to cope with uncertainty, and it also frequently comes.

I further reaffirm that individuals may move from one category to the other, that within each is a range of knowledge and commitment, and that the outer limit of each is apostasy — with or without institutional formalities. Saints who abandon the fellowship of Iron Rods and Liahonas take their private worlds of questions and answers with them. Only the labels lose their relevance.

The second question to which my friends responded after reading my earlier essay and to which I turn now is: How do recent developments in Mormonism look to "people like me"?

Let me begin with an overall generalization. Within the LDS and RLDS churches, we are still some distance from a "unity of the faith," and in institutional terms we are moving in divergent directions. The official voice of the Reorganization sounds enough like a Liahona to give concern to some RLDS Iron Rods, while the authorized voice of the Utah church is more comfortable to those Saints who accept prescribed answers than to those who raise perplexing questions. However, the recent history of the LDS church is far more complex than this one-sentence synopsis suggests.

For one thing, a striking development of the last twenty years is that the Mormon Liahonas have gone public. They recognize each other readily and they fellowship openly in firesides, study groups, and a variety of conferences and symposia. They write for a growing number of publications. When *Dialogue* was an infant "journal of Mormon thought," its survival was often in peril. Now it flourishes in a field of competitors — *Exponent II* and *Sunstone*, being prominent examples. *The Journal of Mormon History* and the *John Whitmer Historical Association Journal* must also be considered. All publish material reflecting a broad range of individual viewpoints, but all clearly qualify as Liahona voices.

Concurrently, the formation of the Mormon History Association in 1966 led the way to organizations of LDS professionals in a number of disciplines — arts and letters, sociology, media arts, and family counseling, among others. While membership ranges across the conservative-to-liberal spectrum, the nature of such activities is to address new questions and reexamine old answers. If one wants to broaden his or her circle of Liahona acquaintances, the gatherings and publications of these organizations provide opportunities matched only by the proliferating Sunstone symposiums.

The church university has grown in enrollment, faculty, athletic prowess, and importance as a forum for dialogue among Liahonas, Iron Rods, and observers of the Mormon scene. Conferences of remarkable scope are sponsored by academic departments and institutes. The annual Women's Conference at Brigham Young University is a reminder that the questions-and-answers business is becoming an equal opportunity employer. And despite its institutional connection, *Brigham Young University Studies* publishes more articles addressing open questions than proposing definitive answers. The debate continues about whether a church-related school can be a great university, but scores of Liahona and Iron Rod professors spend far more time and talent trying to make it so than they do tilting with each other.[7]

It is my conviction that the growth of the Mormon church and the continuing emphasis on education have generated a "critical mass" of Liahonas whose spiritual energy cannot be suppressed. It can be employed in the business of the kingdom or it can be excluded, but it cannot be confined. To be in touch with that energy is an exciting thing for "people like me."

However, many of the Liahonas whom I know best see the recent past as "the day of the Iron Rod." Certain developments in the institutional church offer support for this view.

First are the increasingly strenuous efforts to promote uniformity and conformity in the wards and branches throughout the world. "Correlation" — the Mormon code word for standardization of curricula and elimination of competition and duplication in activities — has an eighty-year history, but only in the last twenty years or so has it been the dominant concept in program building. One result has been the disappearance of many distinctive features of the women's

Relief Society, the Sunday school, and the youth organizations of the church. Another is a collection of committee-generated and committee-screened lesson manuals of singular blandness.

A coincident shift toward Christian fundamentalism is also apparent in the approach to the "standard works" incorporated in missionary plans, lesson manuals, official publications, and the sermons of many General Authorities. The verbal infallibility of the scriptures is not explicitly asserted, and in specific instances—like the story of Adam's rib—it is expressly denied. But the frequent and vigorous admonition to "search the scriptures" for authoritative answers to all gospel-related questions reverses a trend away from literalism in the first half of the twentieth century. One of my correspondents sees the 1979 edition of the Bible, with its mass of computer-generated cross references to other LDS scriptures and Joseph Smith's revision of the King James Bible, as "a serious mistake, since it encourages and facilitates the use of a proof-text method of reading the Bible that will only further diminish our understanding of it."

The constant reminder to "follow the brethren" is another Iron Rod characteristic of the past two decades. Implicit in the concept of living prophets, of course, is the idea that authoritative answers are available through chosen individuals, but the advice to depend upon church leaders for guidance in what to think as well as what to do is more prominent at present than in many past periods of LDS history. The church has not officially adopted the neo-Calvinistic theology or the dogma of prophetic infallibility which have been propounded by some church leaders, but the authoritarian climate gives such doctrinal innovations widespread acceptance among answer-oriented Saints.

The downgrading of the study of church history is a recent expression and—to many Mormons—regrettable consequence of the Iron Rod trend. Access to the rich archival resources of the historical division of the LDS church is more restricted than it was fifteen years ago; the research function of the division has been curtailed; its sponsorship of publications has been discontinued; and one of the most important products of the enterprise, James B. Allen's and Glen M. Leonard's *Story of the Latter-day Saints* (Salt Lake City: Deseret Book, 1976), was permitted to remain out of print for over a decade despite continuing demand. The brouhaha during the early 1980s involving several historians and an apostle who strongly advocated "safe" history came to the attention of most of us.

It is arguable, however, that this accentuation of the authoritarian aspect of Mormonism is no more than a defensive institutional response to secular trends in the world and the internal stresses generated by explosive growth in membership, intercultural differences, and great disparities in living standards, education attainments, and gospel understanding. One letter writer notes the affinity between some Mormons and the Moral Majority: "Persons with Iron Rod mentalities . . . seem to agree that the world is going to hell in a handcart and that the only way to stop it is to establish hard and fast behavioral rules that everyone must obey." Another letter sympathizes with those who wear the mantle of leadership: "The potential for our fragmentation is high. Even the vaunted organizational tightness of the ecclesiastical structure is really fragile. Lack of a widespread bureaucracy and very high turnover at the local level lay the entire church open to the possibility of schisms. . . . We lean against that by emphasizing rhetorically 'follow the prophet,' read the scriptures, etc. We cannot afford to recognize widely how much we follow Liahona because that recognition would encourage it to an unacceptable, dysfunctional degree. Outsiders, and particularly intellectuals, hearing the rhetoric think we are far more constrained, authority-ridden, and channeled in thought and action than we are in fact."

That authoritarianism is pragmatic and not wedded to tradition is well illustrated by significant recent changes which are at least as acceptable to Liahona Saints as to rank-and-file Iron Rod members. The revelation abandoning the policy of withholding priesthood from blacks is the most profound of these. But responsiveness to new circumstances may be seen also in the consolidated meeting schedule, the content of the *Ensign*,[8] a new method for funding chapel construction, a redesign of temple garments, and a relaxation of several restrictions governing sealings for the dead. A study conducted by Correlation Evaluation to discover why so many converts do not remain active in the church—like other data-oriented inquiries now in progress—may have important consequences for programs.

Nothing better illustrates the problems of developing an authoritative response to profound social change than the place of women in the church. The institutional emphasis on male priesthood leadership and traditional family values is easier to express in sermons and sculpture than to apply in a world where Mormon women become psychiatrists and senators, adopt hyphenated names at marriage, and deliver their babies in the presence of their nervous husbands. The tactics of opposition to the Equal Rights Amendment generated a serious backlash among Mormons of both sexes, as did the short-lived experiment in restricting sacrament meeting prayers to priesthood holders. The process of institutional accommodation in this volatile matter is not measured by General Conference endorsements of conventional answers but by the way church publications, social service agencies, and the Brethren as individual counselors deal with unconventional problems.

As we look toward the future, several factors sustain optimism and commitment in people like me.

One is the characteristic of Liahona testimonies which has been consistent since 1967. They find in the gospel sufficient answers to enough important questions to function purposefully in the church without answers to the rest.

The second is the historical record — generally better known among Liahonas than Iron Rods — which shows the tremendous capacity of the institutional church to accommodate new realities. When the mission of the restoration is defined in terms of impact on the lives of people, every program, scripture, and prophetic pronouncement is subject to reconstruction or reinterpretation for the sake of that mission.

Furthermore, the limitations of authoritarian control operate as certainly, and more swiftly, in open communities like the church than in states with plenary power to punish nonconformity. I am indebted to my brother, at the time bishop in the same California ward where the Liahona-Iron Rod concept was first proposed, for an illustration of the point: "Suppose I approached the brethren of the priesthood about home teaching as follows: 'I'm sick and tired of your failing to visit all your families. Any elder or seventy or high priest who doesn't do 100 percent home teaching this month is going to have his district taken away from him. Now get out there and do it!' Do you know how many families the bishopric would be home teaching next month? Two hundred and fifty. (That's one hundred and twenty-five for each counselor.) And at the end of the second month do you know how many counselors the bishop would have? None."

Finally, the trend of the last twenty years has not altered the fact that the church continues to be—as it has always been—a community of Liahona-type and Iron Rod-type believers. During this period my own research has given me a rather intimate acquaintance with two former counselors in the First Presidency—Hugh B. Brown and Henry D. Moyle. One was a Liahona, impatient with dogmatism. The other was an Iron Rod, impatient with opposition. Each was well-leavened with pragmatism, each was disappointed that the institutional church did not follow the path which he would have preferred, and each was unquestionably "true to the faith." The tendencies in Mormonism which they represented did not die with them.

The same correspondent who noted that this is the "day of the Iron Rod" went on to remark: "The division into the two types is virtually universal in the church. Sooner or later, Iron Rods will have to make peace with Liahonas. Else the church will split." Like this good friend—who happens not to be a Latter-day Saint—"I do not expect that to happen." On the contrary, I fully share the conviction of another good friend—a Mormon who knows as much about Liahonas and Iron Rods as anybody: "I have always believed that both can abide each other without difficulty as long as they have the spirit of Christ."

— *Notes* —

1. Robert Gottlieb and Peter Wiley, *America's Saints: The Rise of Mormon Power* (New York: G. P. Putnam's Sons, 1984), 235–36, 238; Leonard J. Arrington and Davis Bitton, *The Mormon Experience: A History of the Latter-day Saints* (New York: Alfred A. Knopf, 1979), 334–35. For citations of the reprintings of the article, see the Introduction.

2. Harold B. Lee, "The Iron Rod," *Ensign* 1 (June 1971): 7. The same sermon quotes with approval the definition: "A liberal in the church is merely one who does not have a testimony."

3. Kent L. Walgren, "Some Sentimental Thoughts on Leaving the Fold," *Dialogue: A Journal of Mormon Thought* 13 (Winter 1980): 75–80.

4. Eugene E. Campbell and Richard D. Poll, *Hugh B. Brown: His Life and Thought* (Salt Lake City: Bookcraft, 1975), 196.

5. A perceptive discussion of how active Latter-day Saints use "obstructionism, pouting, procrastination, intentional inefficiency or stubbornness to reflect the disagreement or hostility one does not express openly"

is K-Lynn Paul, "Passive Aggression and the Believer," *Dialogue: A Journal of Mormon Thought* 10 (Autumn 1977): 86–91.

6. Joseph Smith, *History of the Church of Jesus Christ of Latter-day Saints*, ed. B. H. Roberts, 7 vols. (Salt Lake City: Deseret Book, 1973), 5:135.

7. Three recent episodes — the demise of the *7th East Press*, the termination of Professor David P. Wright, and the resignation of Professor D. Michael Quinn from Brigham Young University — are reminders that freedom of expression is not unlimited.

8. Although the official church magazine carries an aura of authoritarianism, external and internal evidence suggests that a number of its writers are Liahonas. Articles dealing with specific human problems are frequently suggestive rather than prescriptive in tone and sensitive to the complexities of contemporary life which make some traditional answers irrelevant or difficult to apply.

3

God and Man in History

THE CHURCH OF JESUS CHRIST OF LATTER-DAY SAINTS SEES BOTH
God and humanity in a temporal, that is historical, context, but it has
developed no authoritative, systematic statement of the philosophical
implications of historical relationships. It has no *official* philosophy of
history. What follows, therefore, are simply reflections on some problems which relate to the religious affirmations of the LDS people and
a tentative approach to my personal philosophy of history.

By "philosophy of history" I mean a central conception of
what history is about. What does the process add up to? Does it have
meaning? Is it going anywhere? If so, where? Is it going up, down, or
around in a circle, or up and down like a roller coaster? What purposes does history serve? And what are the ultimate ends toward which
it is moving?

In the doctrines of Mormonism there are, of course, many
statements about God, humans, time, matter, space, intelligence, law,
choice, and other subjects which are highly relevant to these questions. However, the integration of these affirmations into a comprehensive and internally consistent philosophy of history has not yet
been accomplished. I am not now attempting to perform that service
for the church but rather to explore a few problems which must be
resolved by whoever undertakes that task.

There are many variant philosophies of history to which people have given intellectual, emotional, and even activist commitment
over the centuries. The late nineteenth century found many Americans committed to what might be called a straight-line progress

philosophy; each generation, standing on the shoulders of its prede-
cessors, was seen as moving toward a more ideal society. The twentieth century shattered many of the philosophical assumptions of inevitable progress, giving rise to such cyclical theories of history as the
secular cycles of Oswald Spengler and the religiously oriented cycles
of Arnold Toynbee. Deterministic philosophies such as Marxism see
social laws leading us inevitably in certain directions, while theolog-
ically based neo-Calvinism predestinates the historical process according to God's will. One fashionable trend is to deny history and philosophy. To some, life started as an accident and has been a combination
of accidents — or "happenings" — ever since. This notion of life as essentially absurd — without fundamental meaning — is found in some versions of existentialism.

Latter-day Saints can find some basis for associating with any
and all of these philosophies, but we have not, as a church, identified
clearly with any of them. And yet the LDS way of looking at life
contains the ingredients for a philosophy of history. The concept of
dispensations lends itself to a cyclical idea, or perhaps a cyclical spi-
ral, with some repetitions from dispensation to dispensation but with
each building upon its predecessor. This cumulative conception of
progress, however, must be set off against the concept of a Golden
Age at the beginning of the human story. Some years ago adult priesthood holders studied a book based upon the notion that the beginning phase was the best phase; it was followed by a series of apostas-
ies and partial restorations by which humanity is gradually working
its way back to the level of the beginning.[1]

The concept of the miraculous in Mormonism has implications for a philosophy of history. It can support the idea of theological determinism — that God is actively directing the historic process
and doing whatever is necessary to accomplish his purposes, whether
making the sun stand still for Joshua or raising Lazarus from the dead.
Occasionally, however, one encounters testimonies of miracles which
suggest a whimsical quality about divine interpositions, like the ancient
Greek philosophies of history in which the gods are directly involved
but seem to be playing pointless games with men and women as pawns.

A mechanistic determinism can be derived from the idea of
irrevocable laws according to which things happen. Even the Lord,
according to Mormon theology, is bound by these laws. We do certain things and certain results occur; they may be blessings or penal-

ties, but they are built into the system. However, many aspects of Mormonism resist such a deterministic conception. The affirmation that humans are free agents — that they have the capacity for real choice — serves as the basis for an indeterministic philosophy of history. Thus, according to some, humans as free agents are going somewhere. While others suggest that humans are merely biding their time, trying to avoid worldly transgressions until the millennial end comes.

Why has the church developed no systematic philosophy of history — no unifying conception about the historical process? For one reason, in our approach to our religion we Latter-day Saints display little sense of history. Apart from the veneration of certain idealized episodes from the past — the first visions, the martyrdom of the prophet, the crossing of the plains — we have forgotten our past. And as far as such features of that past as plural marriage are concerned, some of us would appreciate not being reminded of them.

Not merely the events of the past, but the concept of the past as a process influences current LDS thought very little. The significant legacy of the past is popularly seen as a body of revelations, of encapsulated and uncontested truths which are of equal validity and relevance in every generation. The rest of the historic record is nonfunctional in terms of the quest for exaltation and so, the counsel of Doctrine and Covenants 88 notwithstanding, the body of historical knowledge and experience is not brought to bear on the decisions and value judgments of the here and now.

Let me illustrate this and certain other propositions with some findings from a survey made at Brigham Young University in December 1969. A group of more than 1,500 students in my American Heritage class answered a series of propositions designed to discover what they "*really* think about their educational experience and some of the issues which are periodically discussed" at the university. They responded on a "strongly agree — strongly disagree" five-option scale. The same instrument was used with several other groups for comparison purposes. Two of the propositions illustrate what I believe to be the case — that the typical LDS approach to life today is not tied to an awareness of yesterday.

One of the survey items concerned perceptions of the secular past: "The United States is a less virtuous nation today than it was a century ago." Sixty percent of the survey group, almost all Mormons, agreed, while 20 percent were undecided, and only 20 percent disagreed. The apocalyptic doctrinal view of the last days requires a framework of moral deterioration of society, and even exposure to my mildly optimistic interpretation of the American heritage did not override the historical image which millennarianism almost requires. If one recalls that "a century ago" means the period of the Tweed Ring, Southern Reconstruction, child labor, and the anti-Chinese riots on the Pacific Coast, one is not surprised to note that only one of fourteen graduate students in history who were surveyed and only two of sixteen history professors at BYU agreed with the proposition.

The second proposition concerned historic process within the church: "Some LDS doctrines have changed since Joseph Smith's day." Forty percent agreed, while 20 percent were undecided, and 40 percent disagreed. By contrast, only three of the graduate history majors and one of the history faculty members disagreed with the proposition. To the extent that the oracles from the past are perceived as unchanging, the processes of change — of continuous revelation — within the church today are likely to be resisted, overlooked, or rationalized away.

Let me comfort other Mormon historians by suggesting that the American Heritage survey did not confirm the occasionally voiced suspicion that the study of history leads to apostasy. None of the propositions used in the survey was, in fact, a definitive gospel concept, although some of them had dogmatic advocacy among Latter-day Saints who feel some need to define church positions in areas where the voice of revelation is silent. Rather, the results of the survey seemed to confirm the general truth that intellectual inquiry can be disturbing to conventional and traditional wisdom.

Having thus paid respects to the explanation that we Latter-day Saints have no systematic philosophy of history because we have little sense of the nature and relevance of history, let me argue next that, to this date, the LDS church has no systematic theology. Courses in the church's institutes and private schools, for example, discuss the nature of time, evil, knowledge, humanity, truth, and reality; but one finds therein no set of systematic propositions which may be followed by the phrase, "Thus saith the Lord." The addresses and writings of the General Authorities offer a number of excellent precepts for living and some ideas about the nature of life that give meaning to those precepts. They also contain affirmations about the remote past and

the remote future, but they can be fitted into a wide range of philosophical systems. One need only live for a while on the BYU campus
and hear ultimate reality defined in a half-dozen different courses by
a half-dozen different professors, some of them professional theolo-
gians and all of them committed Latter-day Saints, to discover a range
of philosophic preferences which approaches anarchy.

This lack of consensus was reflected in the American Heritage survey, in which one item invited agreement or disagreement
with the proposition: "Man is by nature evil." Among the 1,500 under-
graduates, mostly freshmen, 68 percent said, "No." Among the recently
returned missionaries, 51 percent said, "No," while more than 80 percent of the graduate students and history faculty were in the negative,
apparently preferring the "as God once was" to the "carnal, sensual,
and devilish" theme in Mormon teachings about humanity.

Latter-day Saints have difficulty with such basic conceptions
as the nature of time and space, the ultimate stages upon which the
historic process unfolds. Most of the talk about eternity and infinity
simply proceeds from the assumption that humans are here on a plan-
etary piece of matter, moving through God's universe. We are at the
center, time going infinitely forward and backward and space going
endlessly in all directions from this point. For the serious and perplexing implications of such concepts as eternity and infinity, there is
little concern. We have as much time and space as anybody else, and
the important question is what we are doing with them.

Certainly when it comes to the fundamental conception of
the relationship between God, our Heavenly Father, and time and
space, one finds a wide range of opinion. The topic, "God and Man in
History," is consistent with Mormonism in suggesting that God is *in*
the historical process. This is in contradistinction to Catholicism and
certain other theologies which hold that God, by very nature, is outside the time and space context; all things are simultaneously present
with him and the passing of time is only with us. Yet many Mormons
want both the security that comes from the concept of a Supreme
Being who is apart from the temporal process and the feeling of kinship which comes from a Heavenly Father who is involved somehow
in the same process as humans — who in some way *was* once as we are
now and who *is* now as we may someday become. The ostensibly
authoritative discourses on this subject convey a strong suggestion
that in this matter we can eat our cake and have it too.

On the American Heritage survey the highest degree of consensus was achieved on the proposition relevant at this point: "God is
all-knowing, all powerful, and unchanging." In the total class sample, 85 percent agreed, with returned missionaries two points higher.
Yet among seniors in the sample, the affirmative percentage was only
80, and 110 seniors in the Honors Program registered 70 percent. What
of the history faculty? They divided nine to four for the *negative*, with
three undecided; for the majority of this sample of LDS professionals
in history, God is *in* time with them.

This basic question of the relationship of God to time is cru-
cially related to the question of his relationship to prophecy. Is the
future to God as the future is to his children or has the future already
arrived as far as he is concerned? In what sense does God know the
future? Raised in any local priesthood quorum, this question may
receive as many answers as priesthood bearers present. Is the future
absolutely present, absolutely certain, in the mind of the Lord? Or is
the future known to him because, as an earthly father knows what his
children are likely to do, so our Heavenly Father is able to look ahead,
diagnose, and predict? Does the Lord in fact foresee the future on the
basis of superior predictive knowledge, or is his knowledge of the
future absolute because he has a different relationship to that future
than we do? Again, there is no consensus among Latter-day Saints.

So too with a closely related question, fundamental to an
approach to history: Is the future fixed for anyone? Some scriptures
state that the end is known from the beginning and that some of the
prophets saw the end from the beginning. Yet we are also taught that
what happens today can affect what happens tomorrow; we are not
just role playing but making choices, and our choices make a difference.

Almost every Mormon will accept the proposition that what
an individual does has a bearing on his or her own personal salvation.
But that is a different thing from saying that what one does not only
affects his or her own future but bears on the outcome of the whole
enterprise in which we are collectively engaged. A fairly prevalent
view sees the Lord so closely managing this world that no individual
choice affects the larger process; the erring soul will be left with the
consequences of a mistake, but the total story of humankind will proceed to exactly the same foreordained end as if the sinner had not
taken the wrong turn in the road.

On this crucial question, the Saints range as widely as it is possible to range. Some cherish a hard-shelled Calvinistic theology which makes humans little more than pawns who have the illusion of choice but in fact do what they have been foreordained to do. Such Mormons reject the wicked word "predestination" but accept the content of the word because it satisfies the yearning for historical certainty. Some express their tendencies toward authoritarianism and their yearnings for an unchanging God in conceptions of history almost Catholic. Other church members espouse liberal ideas of historical progression through meaningful human choices. Their emphasis on a social gospel makes free agency a key not only to individual exaltation but to the outcome for humankind in this telestial world. Still others become so harassed and bewildered that they talk in strong pessimistic terms: what happens does not make much difference, really. We are just muddling up the Lord's program; may he soon cut short the whole painful business!

In such perplexity and diversity lies grist for much interesting if rarely rigorous discussion, but nothing which emerges can appropriately be represented as *the* church philosophy of history. No Latter-day Saint Thomas, Bossuet, Hegel, or Marx has made an acceptable synthesis, nor does the lack of such a synthesis cause much concern.

The conclusion of this commentary on the theme, "God and Man in History," does not attempt an institutionalized Mormon philosophy then but merely presents some thoughts on how one LDS historian handles some of the questions of faith which stem from his vocation. Let us look at first things first.

God seems to me to be present in history in these ways:

In the first place he organized the enterprise out of whatever was there before — ideas, intelligence, energy, matter — and he involved us in it. He understands the process and the goals, and he defines those goals to us to the extent that he can get through to us and we to him. There is then purpose in the process; history *is* going *somewhere*.

Further, the Lord directs and influences the outcome of that process. This intervention, however, is not analogous to one of those clocks which, when they run one second fast or slow, are automatically corrected by some mechanical or electrical means. The intervention of our Heavenly Father is not that coercive or continuous; it is sufficient to keep the process related to the goals. Suppose a prophet misses his calling, leaving an important task undone. Somehow the job will get done. But there may well be some slippage in the process; the task may not be done quite so neatly and expeditiously if ground has to be recovered.

Divine intervention is to be expected at points where that intervention is indispensable for God's purposes to be fulfilled. The key intervention is the atonement brought to pass through Jesus Christ, a historical event in which something that had to be done and could not be done otherwise was miraculously done. There are other key areas in which the conditions have required interposition, such as the opening of dispensations. (For purposes of this analysis, consideration of private miracles is omitted, although their relevance to some points in the discussion will be apparent.)

With regard to the relationship of God to the future and the outcome of the historic process, they are known to him only in generalized terms because, in fact, they are being worked out within the context of time. This seems to me inescapable. If the historic process is in fact being worked out by meaningful choices—if something that happens can make a real difference in what happens next—then the ultimate outcome can only be clear in general terms to anyone—God or humans—who functions within that process.

I will not argue with the proposition that the Lord *can* direct events so that at every point he will be in command of what is happening and it will come out exactly right. For reasons to be considered presently, I do not see this as the way God has defined his role. But even if he were to give such close and coercive direction, it would not be based upon a detailed knowledge of the end from the beginning but upon the possession of sufficient power to relate decisively to the unfolding sequence of events. For if he is in fact living in time— if he is in any sense a progressing entity—then the future is ahead for him. He masters eternity as he uses knowledge to master the historic process, which is eternal.

This concept of God's relation to history helps to explain the inefficiency of the historic process as perceived by the historian. Given the power which is the Lord's, there ought to be a better way of saving humanity, if reaching the foreordained end were the only goal of life. There is too much wasteful loss of human effort and potential, not from the sins that contribute somehow to learning and possible growth but from pointless evil—the mountains that slide down and bury scores of school children before they have a chance to savor the opportunities of life. Mormons handle such problems of gratuitous evil in different ways, but it seems to me that involved here is the centrality of freedom in the historic process, a process to which our Heavenly Father is committed partly by his nature and partly by his will. Bound by his temporal nature and by the laws of the space in which he functions, God further restrains the arbitrary use of his knowledge of these laws in order that humans may grow by learning those same laws and making wise choices based upon them. That is one reason why the historic process cannot be precisely plotted and why it is as inefficient, painful, and pathetic as it is.

This view of God in history also helps us to understand the relationship between prophecy and history. When reading the language of recorded prophecy, one finds some language that reads almost like history and some that does not. We find also that the prophecies with the most specific and clearly identifiable referents deal with the prophet's own day and time, while those which relate to the remoter future do so in more generalized terms. If a hundred years hence is as clear to prophetic insight as a hundred years ago, this should not be the case.[2]

This point can be illustrated by any number of prophetic foreshadowings of the last days, not only in the Old and New Testaments but also in other LDS scriptures. Graphic in imagery and warning, they defy precise identification with unfolding events while tantalizing scriptorians of every generation to make the attempt. Also illustrative is the prophecy (D&C 87) on the Civil War, often cited as an example of Joseph Smith's inspired gifts. Written in 1832, it begins with specific allusions to South Carolina's rebellion against the tariff and Nat Turner's slave rebellion, both then in the news, but as it looks farther ahead the language becomes so broad that it cannot yet be confidently said to what extent it has come to pass. In 1862 Brigham Young said that the prophecy was being fulfilled with the pending destruction of the Union; by 1865, the Civil War being over, he had come to another conclusion.

A plausible, and to me persuasive, explanation of this aspect of prophecy is that the future cannot be described with complete precision because that precision depends upon what happens between prediction and fulfillment. The combination of circumstances, from the time that Isaiah foresaw the coming of a messiah down to the time when John the Baptist baptized Jesus and to the time when the post-meridian disciples of Christ wrote what had happened, conditioned what each *could* write. The farther one looks into the future, even under divine inspiration, the more generalized he or she must necessarily be, because the future is not yet fact.

This is the way one historian with an LDS commitment handles the problem of the relationship of God to the historic process. It is a directing and ultimately controlling participation but one which is limited in part by the nature of our Heavenly Father himself and partly by his commitment to the free agency of men and women.

Which leads to the question of the role of humans in history.

The initial assumption is that humans as free agents are co-eternal with God and so are a meaningful part of the whole historic process. We can easily cast ourselves in the role of enemies, but we are meant to be partners with the Lord. What we do makes a difference in the outcome of history.

For one thing, what we do affects the timetable of revelation as far as the Lord is concerned. We are repeatedly reminded that one of the reasons we do not receive more light is that we are not making much use of the light we now have. If we were to do so, it would have real bearing on what God would be contributing to the historic process.

In the second place, what we do significantly affects the timetable of progress. Both in the meridian dispensation and in the dispensation of our day, the prophet-leaders who opened them up were optimistic about how much time it would take to complete the work. This is a possible explanation for the statements by Joseph Smith and some of his associates, as well as some New Testament prophets, which were interpreted by members of the church as meaning that the Second Coming was an immediate prospect. The prophets were overwhelmed by the manifestations of the power of God and the beauty of the gospel; surely no one could resist. But the capacity of humans to resist the counsel of the Lord is depressingly apparent in every dispensation. So it takes more time than the prophets hoped, and as a rather wry fact of the Dispensation of the Fullness of Times, most Mormons in this generation are less confident of the immediacy of the Second Coming than were Joseph Smith's contemporaries.

LDS diversity on this point is graphically revealed in another item from the American Heritage survey. To the proposition: "The

Millennium will begin within the next fifty years," 50 percent of the large class agreed, 40 percent registered indecision, and 10 percent disagreed. Among the experts (our historian sample), the crystal ball was also clouded, but a clear majority was undecided or answered in the negative. I suggest that some of the ambiguity with which we Latter-day Saints relate to the problems of our secular society stems from this indecision about the temporal implications of the phrase, "the latter days."[3]

Under the circumstances, some people legitimately think that certain things need to be done — an acceptable amount of preaching of the gospel, of work for the dead, of building temples, of gathering, and of various kinds of good deeds — as conditions for the Second Coming. A certain amount of trouble is also foreseen, but any reading of history presents sufficient calamity in every generation, including our own, so there need be no stirring up of woe to fulfill the gloomier prophecies of the pre-millennial finale. The tempo of events, in any case, is not decreed.

By this conception of the role of humans in the historic process, we not only save or lose ourselves by our acts, with the indispensable assistance of Jesus Christ, but have influence on the timetable and the details of the larger story. Into this context fits the scripture, "The day and the hour no man knoweth, not even the angels in heaven, but my Father only" (Matt. 24:36). Some people say this means that the Lord is keeping it a secret from everyone, but it can also be read as meaning that, within certain tolerances known only to God, it could go one way or another. If all people would repent and really act repentant, the story could be concluded in a few years. Or perhaps H-bombs could be used to create an environment which would make the finale indispensable. The conclusion is the same: We do have something to do with the apocalyptic schedule — the point at which and the circumstances in which this phase of the historic process ends.

The sum of the matter for this LDS writer is that the history of humanity is not already written, not even for the Lord himself. What we are presently engaged in is not a drama without a point or a fortuitous comedy of errors or a foredoomed tragedy or a fully scripted pageant in which we are all mimes. Fundamental to this concept is the conviction that God is the producer and Jesus Christ is the central actor in the play, but what happens on the stage depends significantly upon the choices of all members of the cast.

The study of the past is thus profitable for Latter-day Saints and commended by scripture (D&C 88:79). Study of the record of our forbears' deeds may help us better to discharge our responsibilities toward that chapter of the eternal sage being written by our own generation. As John F. Kennedy put it in his inaugural address: "With a good conscience our only sure reward, with history the final judge of our deeds, let us go forward to lead the land we love, asking his blessing and his help but knowing that, here on earth, God's work must truly be our own."

— *Notes* —

1. Milton R. Hunter, *The Gospel Through the Ages* (Salt Lake City: Deseret Book, 1945).

2. The observable differences between Old Testament prophecies about the coming of a messiah and Book of Mormon prophecies about the coming of Jesus Christ may, it is suggested, be attributed at least in part to the fact that the latter-day translator of the Book of Mormon knew, on the basis of historical information, some of the things which had happened in the interim and so could relate the prophecies rather specifically to events which satisfied their terms; hence Jesus comes through much more clearly in Alma than in Isaiah. No comparable differences are found in the way the two scriptures deal with the still-future millennial dispensation. (This interpretation is based on the further assumption that Joseph Smith's translating went to the meaning of his sources rather than to the individual English equivalents of ancient symbols.)

3. The absence of an LDS consensus on major social issues was illustrated in these responses on the American Heritage survey. There is no evidence that the same propositions, or comparable statements about child care programs, drug testing, or nuclear disarmament, would discover consensus today.

Proposition	Agree	Undecided	Disagree
Peaceful coexistence between the U.S. and the U.S.S.R. is possible.	49%	16%	35%
The war in Vietnam is an immoral war.	27%	23%	50%
The Supreme Court ruling against required prayers in public schools is wrong.	49%	17%	34%

Proposition	Agree	Undecided	Disagree
A capitalistic economic system functions best when it is regulated by government.	44%	31%	25%
Sex education does not belong in the public schools.	41%	18%	41%

The impression conveyed by these responses (December 1969) was of an opinion configuration more conservative than that likely to be encountered in other large universities but hardly indicative of a doctrinally imposed unanimity. No correlations were run between strength of millennial expectations and views on contemporary public issues, but the survey responses as a whole supported the not-surprising conclusion that among Latter-day Saints, as in many other religious groups, theological fundamentalism is associated with political conservatism.

4

The Happy Valley Syndrome

IN THE FIRST OF THE TWO NEW TESTAMENT LETTERS ATTRI-
buted to the apostle Peter there appears a description of the Church
of Christ that has presented a challenge to believers in all generations
and provides a text for my inquiry into certain traits of the present
Mormon generation: "But ye are a chosen generation, a royal priesthood, an holy nation, a peculiar people; that ye should shew forth the
praises of him who hath called ye out of darkness into his marvelous
light" (2:9).

The phrase "a peculiar people" appears in both Old and New
Testaments but with somewhat different connotations. In Deuter-
onomy (14:2; 26:18) it is found in context with Hebraic law and ritual,
and the implication is that the chosen people should be visibly distinctive and apart from other nations. In Peter, on the other hand, as
in Titus 2:4, the peculiarity is a quality of relationship with the world—
a relationship which recalls other scriptural passages such as "light
on a hill" and "salt of the earth" (D&C 86:11; 101:16; 115:5). To be "in
the world but not of the world" meant both physical and psychological segregation to ancient Israel; it meant a ministry of light among
nations in darkness to the disciples of the Lord.

That the preoccupations of some Latter-day Saints today suggest an Old Testament rather than a New Testament concept of "a
peculiar people" is my present thesis and concern.

The "Happy Valley Syndrome" is that collection of traits
which tends to make some of us Mormons isolated and odd—clois-
tering together against the tribulations of the world outside and

41

identifying exaltation with verbal affirmations and habitual, group-reinforced forms of righteousness.[1] I do not mean here to associate the syndrome with any particular person, living or dead. One or more of the symptoms are present in many Latter-day Saints, and my hope is that if self-examination leads to recognition, the temptation to repent will not be resisted.

Let us pause here to define terms. One dictionary explains that a syndrome is "a group of signs or symptoms that appear together and characterize a particular abnormality." My own definition of "Happy Valley" is the cultural enclave within which many Latter-day Saints believe that security exists and may be expected to continue to exist as long as firm resistance is maintained against impinging forces from the outside world.

Three signs or symptoms collectively characterize this Happy Valley Syndrome for Latter-day Saints. They are (1) a marginal awareness of past reality, (2) a myopic perspective on present reality, and (3) a mechanical approach to divine reality. A concept of spiritual security focused on formalized abstractions and ritualized actions builds barriers between Syndrome-Saints and the world in which they live, the historic influences and processes that shaped it, and the God in whose hands is its destiny — and theirs.

By minimal awareness of past reality, I mean that many Latter-day Saints have little or no sense of history. My belief that studying the past is helpful in relating to the present and the future reflects more than professional bias, but I will not undertake its systematic validation here. I will simply observe that no historical understanding or perspective is involved in the way many of us relate religious beliefs to the current business of living. A narrow illustration is the genealogist who collects names without attention to the context within which the bearers of the names lived. A broader and more serious manifestation is the way we appeal to a past that never was. History is alleged to "prove" many things that history almost certainly does not prove. For example, most of the "reasons," based on *a priori* generalizations, about "why Rome fell" are allegations for which there is little or no real support.

I am particularly concerned about our loss of a sense of history as far as our church is concerned. Many of us seem to be unaware of the long, dynamic historical process which has brought us to the

present day. We cherish mythologized memories about certain locations — the sacred grove, the Kirtland temple, the red brick store and
the temple in Nauvoo, and Winter Quarters. But we sing "Come,
Come, Ye Saints," with its conclusion that for all who made it to the
valley or died on the way, "all is well, all is well," as though that is
where our history ends. The great scholarly writings about Mormon
history, of which Leonard Arrington's *Great Basin Kingdom*
(Cambridge: Harvard University Press, 1958) is a path-breaking example, are not widely read by the people for whom LDS historians write
them. The processes of change and development traced in B. H.
Roberts's great *Comprehensive History of the Church* (Salt Lake City:
Deseret News Press, 1930) and more recently and succinctly in James
B. Allen's and Glen B. Leonard's *The Story of the Latter-day Saints* (Salt
Lake City: Deseret Book, 1976) are unknown to many Mormons.
Today's church is assumed to be what the pioneers brought with them
in 1847, costumed differently and communicating by satellite.

Yesterday was not the same as today, and today is not what
tomorrow will be. Yet most of us are unfamiliar with the fact that
almost revolutionary institutional changes followed the decision to
abandon polygamy and political isolationism.[2] I mention this not to
encourage the accumulation of historical trivia for quiz programs but
because awareness of the possibilities for change is essential to relating constructively to the processes of change. The Ninth Article of
Faith suggests that change will be the essence of this dispensation, as
new truth is added to that which has previously been available to the
Saints. Yet when we use authorities to establish points of doctrine and
to define policies, we quote with no regard for the historical context
or particular relevance of the sources used. Old Testament prophet
Ezekiel and Book of Mormon prophet Alma are as authoritative for
formulating decisions on current church curricula — or American politics — as quotations from church presidents John Taylor or Lorenzo
Snow or statements from the prophets of our own day.

Furthermore, we seem to resist the *idea* of institutional change
in the church, even though the past is full of it and we readily accommodate it when it occurs. Who among today's Latter-day Saints knows
that fast day was observed on Thursday during most of the nineteenth
century? Among those who are old enough to remember when the
sacrament was administered in Sunday school, who knows that the
ordinance was *not* part of the early format of that teaching institution?

Who knows that elders were once ordained at such tender ages as thirteen and fourteen? Now that all but two of the quorums of seventies have disappeared, who is aware that membership in the First Quorum of the Seventy was once restricted to seventies and that some of them, like B. H Roberts, took seriously the affirmation in Doctrine and Covenants 107:26 that the quorum was equal in authority to the Council of the Twelve Apostles?

These kinds of institutional changes, some of them quite significant, continue to go on all around us. For example, the churchwide and worldwide implications of the 1978 revelation on blacks and the priesthood are immeasurable.

To the extent we cling to the perception that the Restoration consists of a package of revealed and uncontexted principles, policies, and practices, given to the prophet Joseph Smith and meant to be preserved intact until the Millennium, we may occasionally be startled, even upset, by changes, but we can have no influence upon their nature, direction, or tempo.

Let me share an incident which illustrates how institutional change can take place in this church. A generation ago, when our daughters were in the children's Primary and young adult Mutual Improvement Association stages, the Polls and another couple became concerned about the promotion system being used between the two auxiliaries. At that time the Aaronic Priesthood analogy was being followed, with the girls going into MIA one at a time, on their twelfth birthday. This seemed to weaken the impact of both the last year in Primary and the first in MIA. If a divine purpose was being served by following the boys' pattern, then obviously we ought to adjust, but it did not appear to us that this was so. We respectfully raised the question with the general boards of the two auxiliaries, and soon we were on a committee appointed by them and were conducting a churchwide survey. Within a few months the policy was changed, girls began to be promoted at the end of the program year, and the Polls and their friends were rewarded with certificates naming them honorary members of the two general boards. (After about twenty-five years the one-at-a-time promotion policy was reinstated. I do not know whether this change should be attributed to providential intervention, cumulative experience, other parental activism, or church correlation.)

I mention this only to illustrate an important, incontrovertible point. Some of the changes that have made the church a more efficient and effective influence in the lives of its members have been responsive to grassroots input like this. If individual members feel that their only responsibility is to relate passively and obediently to whatever the institutional status quo requires, they overlook the free agency factor in the principle of common consent. Or they exercise it — as many of us do — by griping to peers or engaging in passive resistance, both of which are indirect ways of producing change.

While censuring these negative activities in a thoughtful address on "Criticism," Apostle Dallin H. Oaks recently endorsed the private communication of concerns and suggestions about church policies and programs to those who are in a position to act upon them. "Our Father in Heaven has not compelled us to think the same way on every subject or procedure. As we seek to accomplish our life's purposes, we will inevitably have differences with those around us — including some of those we sustain as our leaders. The question is not whether we have such differences, but how we manage them. . . . By following these procedures, Church members can work for correction of a leader or for change in a policy" (*Ensign* 18 [Feb. 1987]: 72).

The Mormon church today is in important ways a product of its history, and the church fifty years from now, whether or not the Millennium has come, will be in part a product of what happens in this generation. Surely awareness of what, where, when, how, and why past changes have occurred will not disqualify us from constructive involvement in today's dynamic church. It may even make us more profitable servants.

Let us turn now to the second symptom of the Happy Valley Syndrome — myopic perspective on present reality. There is some evidence that what some Latter-day Saints profess as the gospel is detached from the real world in which we live, move, and have our being. Preoccupied with what we have defined as the business of salvation, we are uninterested and uninformed about the problems of the world beyond the valley and apathetic in the discharge of our civic responsibilities.

This is not an appeal to emulate the violence of much social protest but rather a challenge to make our Christian commitment a significant conditioning factor as we define — just for ourselves, not for the church — positions on the crucial issues of today. As we take our stands on law and order, urban decay, education, national defense, and public revenue priorities, it seems to me that gospel principles ought to be distinctively and conspicuously present in the way we reach conclusions and then act upon them. Instead, many of us pick up our opinions from the Rotary Club, the union hall, or the evening news, or we parrot the opinions of ecclesiastical or secular leaders whose status or general philosophy appeals to us.

Let me illustrate this problem with an experiment I once did in two large classes in American history. As part of each weekly quiz I asked opinion questions about current affairs, partly to get an idea of what the students were thinking and partly to provoke more thinking. Usually the opinion questions were identical for both classes; this time, however, there was a difference. The first group was asked: "What is your opinion of the statement, 'There is enough good in the United Nations to justify its existence'?" With five choices, about 16 percent strongly agreed, 45 percent agreed, 20 percent had no opinion, and almost 20 percent chose the negative options. The second group was asked: "What is your opinion of this statement by David O. McKay, 'There is enough good in the United Nations to justify its existence'?" You can predict the outcome. This time approximately 35 percent strongly agreed, another 45 percent agreed, only 10 percent were undecided, and the negatives had dwindled to about 7 percent.

My concern was not about whether there was or was not "good in the United Nations" but about the tendency among us to let authority figures make up our minds for us. On gospel topics deferring to authority is safe — and usually sound — policy, but the merits or demerits of the United Nations are not yet elements of gospel doctrine or church policy. They are matters about which we are entirely free to exercise our free agency. I recommend that we all make a greater effort to define our own relationships, as believing and practicing Latter-day Saints, to the institutions and issues of the secular world that will profoundly affect us and our children.

Another aspect of this second symptom is that, apart from certain church practices which might almost be regarded as eccentricities, most Mormons relate to the problems of the world in about the same fashion as their Gentile contemporaries of comparable economic and social status. In community service, the Latter-day Saint may be the one who does not serve coffee at the PTA board meeting or the one who can't come to a board meeting because she has a conflicting Relief Society meeting. But how, as a PTA board member, does she relate to problems in a discernibly different way? Does the leaven of the gospel give her a "peculiar" perspective on school curriculum, boundaries, or bussing?

Sociologists, psychologists, and political scientists—Mormons among them—have discovered that BYU students break traffic rules and get into sexual mischief in ways not so different from their non-Mormon contemporaries as differences in dogma would seem to require. Before the 1978 revelation of priesthood eligibility, one of our sociologists undertook to measure Mormon attitudes on racial differences. The best he could establish on the basis of sound survey techniques was that we were just about as bigoted as everybody else; the priesthood policy had not made us more bigoted.[3]

Nonetheless, another classroom discussion—this in a small, upper division honors course—revealed that racial bias was surely present. We were discussing a Supreme Court decision on "open housing." I set up a hypothetical case, based on the fact that the Poll house in Provo's Oak Hills neighborhood was on the market. "Suppose that Geneva Steel should bring in a black scientist for their by-products lab, and he heard that my house was for sale and offered to buy it. Should I sell it to him?" We talked about it at length, in just about the same terms as anybody else in the American middle class would talk about it then. What would the neighbors think? What would happen to real estate values? What about racial intermingling and the possibility that the scientist's son might marry the girl next door? Some of these bright young people thought that I should sell, and some that I shouldn't. Then I suggested a change in the hypothetical situation. "Let's say that the owner of the house is not Richard Poll, but Jesus. Would he sell?" Of course the discussion quickly fell apart, for there was no argument when the case was put in these terms.

What I am suggesting is that many of us Latter-day Saints do not put the problems of the world in these Christian terms. We relate to them as if the gospel had no relevance. We play some conventional civic role, or we play no role at all. One manifestation of the Happy Valley Syndrome is a belief that if one wishes to remain unspotted from the world, he or she should not get involved in the world's business. Utah Valley has a higher percentage of active Mormons than any other metropolitan area, yet both political parties have a dearth of strong candidates for public offices, and seats on community service councils sometimes go begging. Whether Jesus, were he here today, would be a Republican or a Democrat is something to debate at another time. That he would be moved to action by the plight of many of his Father's children is, in my view, undeniable.

My appeal is for an enlargement of our sense of responsibility for trying to make this world a better place. Even if we believe it is ultimately a doomed enterprise, we and our children are going to have to live in it, and anything we can do to ameliorate our circumstances would seem to make sense. I have no doubt that such efforts will be accounted unto us for righteousness when the final reckoning is made. And as we become involved, we should constantly ask ourselves, "How, as a believer in the gospel of Jesus Christ, *should* I relate to this problem?" Generally we are great—active, caring, serving—in dealing with the church members who live in our Happy Valley. I urge a broader concern about those whom the Savior had in mind when he gave us the Parable of the Good Samaritan.

Now to the third aspect of the syndrome—its routinizing effect on our relationship with our Heavenly Father.

The Happy Valley Syndrome is characterized by a defining of righteousness in terms of specific acts that can be confidently labeled "righteousness" because they are spelled out in precise commandments, procedures, rituals, and verbal affirmations. We often manifest this quirk in Sunday school, priesthood quorum meetings, and Relief Society discussions on the topic, "What must we do to be saved?" We list about forty-seven items on the board, all of which are specific acts that are to be performed once in a lifetime (like baptism) or periodically (like going to the temple) or monthly (like paying fast offerings) or weekly (like going to meetings on Sunday). Then, sensing that something is missing, we end the list with some nebulous phrase like "Live a good life." We rarely discuss it, even though this is, in the last analysis, the requirement upon which the efficacy of all the institutionalized, ritualized forms of righteousness depends.

How does our relationship to our Heavenly Father enter into this?

It seems to me that despite a great deal of classroom and pulpit rhetoric about relying on the Spirit and following its prompting, in broad areas of "living a good life" most of us do not really do so.[4] In choosing a vocation, a political party, a car, or a mate, if we make it a matter of prayer at all, it is usually after we have made up our minds.

We then ask for divine confirmation, and usually our prayers are answered; this is the car to buy or the girl to marry. When our need is for understanding about the gospel, its principles or applications, we select the scriptures or consult the General Authorities that we like best. Then we pray about it and our prayer is answered; we were right all the time. We do not, in our prayer posture, express toward our Heavenly Father the sense of dependence which is the real essence of prayer. An acknowledgement of inadequacy, a placing of ourselves humbly in the hands of the Lord, is not our conventional prayer style. No, we pray for support and success for whatever we have already decided is best.

Depending upon God in situations for which the church has not provided neat answers is something all of us could do more. Too many LDS testimonies include facile, glib rejoicing that the Lord is on our side. He does things for us which he does not do for other mortals, because we are his people. Sometimes we read the scriptural promise, "I, the Lord, am bound" to mean that *because* we are Latter-day Saints, God *has* to love us more.

One of the hardest things for us to do is worship. We do not know how to feel and express a profound sense of dependence, a sense of the distance — in knowledge and power — between us and our Heavenly Father. It is a wonderful doctrine that we are gods in embryo, with potential to become perfect, even as he is. But to the extent that we feel that prize to be nearly won, we impede worship. To the extent that we think of God in terms of a kindly schoolteacher, a family doctor, an interstellar mailman, or a celestial Santa Claus, we blaspheme.

The prayer for help when we do not know the way, the prayer for help when there may not be an easy way, the prayer in time of real tragedy — these are the hardest for us to muster. Some of us who are content with affirmations of testimony and expressions of formalized thanks while things are going well in Happy Valley are shattered when confronted by adversity for which neat formulas do not provide explanation.

What I am suggesting is that we all carefully examine the nature of our communication with our Heavenly Father. What *does* happen when we pray? How often do we pray in ways other than the verbal formulations for specific occasions which we learned while growing up?

This is not meant to disparage ritual prayers. They have their place in ritual situations. If a Latter-day Saint had attended the 1787 constitutional convention, the delegates would not have had to turn down Benjamin Franklin's prayer proposal for lack of money to hire a minister. Someone there would have been glad to provide daily prayers without purse or scrip. But if they were as prolix and banal as what we often hear, would they have attracted more divine attention than Franklin's simple acknowledgement of need?

Years ago I encountered this perceptive aphorism: "The function of religion is to comfort the afflicted and afflict the comfortable." The Happy Valley Syndrome is commonly found among the comfortably religious. It is by no means unique to Mormons, but it is sufficiently prevalent among us to obscure and distort what we see when we look backward—to our past, outward—to the world beyond our valley, and upward—to the Lord, from whence cometh our hope.

Is it desirable for us to escape from Happy Valley? Maybe not. The sequestered life offers a kind of security lost to those who engage the lone and dreary world. A person can move a long way toward the personal goal of exaltation by operating in a Happy Valley context as virtuously as he knows he ought to. Most of us, alas, do not even do that.

By the standards defined by Jesus Christ and all the prophets, even "doing that" is not enough.

Let us, as part of our commitment as Latter-day Saints, face the reality of our past, seeking understanding of the processes by which the unfolding of the divine plan has so far come to pass, so that we can relate constructively to present developments, trends, and possibilities.

Let us seek to apply the gospel of love—the gospel of Jesus Christ—in our relations with *all* who are our brothers and sisters, including some who are particularly difficult to love because they have such weird beliefs or live in such squalid circumstances or do such obnoxious things.

Let us confront the inadequacy of the pat answers and comfortable procedures of the cloistered life, so that in humility we may reach out to our Heavenly Father for help in developing the spiritual resources, insights, resolution, courage, and strength to live as our religion really requires.

It is my conviction that as we seek inspiration and try to live in love, we can find in the restored gospel what we need to be worthy servants — worthy children — of our Heavenly Father. He is available to us through the example and teachings of his Son and through the ministry of the Holy Spirit. I pray that we may so respond that we will truly be a "peculiar people," not in the Old Testament sense — isolated and uninvolved — but in the New Testament sense — a leaven in the lump, a light on a hill.

— *Notes* —

1. In his paper, "The Happy Valley Concept," Leonard J. Arrington noted that Dr. Samuel Johnson used the phrase "Happy Valley" in his philosophical novel *Rasselas, or the Prince of Abyssinia* (1759). In serial format, *Rasselas* appeared in *The Improvement Era* in 1906-1907, and the phrase has been used for some time in Cache Valley, Utah Valley, and other Latter-day Saint communities, as well as applied to the University of Massachusetts at Amherst and other academic environments. Johnson's "Happy Valley" was an ideal community, which his hero finally came to appreciate after seeking a more interesting and exciting lifestyle elsewhere in the world.

2. See Thomas G. Alexander, *Mormonism in Transition: A History of the Latter-day Saints, 1890-1930* (Urbana: University of Illinois Press, 1986).

3. Armand L. Mauss, "Mormonism and the Negro: Faith, Folklore, and Civil Rights," *Dialogue: A Journal of Mormon Thought* 2 (Winter 1967): 35-38. The minimal resistance to President Kimball's 1978 revelation would seem encouraging evidence that earlier racial antipathies were not deeply ingrained in most members of the church.

4. In recent years "following the spirit" has received new emphasis among Latter-day Saints. The dogmatic form in which this emphasis sometimes finds expression — a blend of mystical, emotional, fundamentalist, and authoritarian elements — is discussed in O. Kendall White, *Mormon Neo-Orthodoxy: A Crisis Theology* (Salt Lake City: Signature Books, 1987).

5

Of Ignorance and Action

I TAKE AS MY TEXT TWO QUOTATIONS THAT I HAVE USED IN AT
least a hundred college courses. One is a call for action. The other is a
word of caution about how — and how not — to respond to that call.

The first comes from Edmund Burke: "The only thing necessary for the triumph of evil is that good men do nothing." I believe
that many people place too much responsibility for the human predicament upon the evil designs of cunning and crafty men and women.
I suggest that they are abetted in their designs by good people who
do not know how to express the goodness they feel within themselves. So they do nothing.

If we resolve to act against the evil in this world, then the
second quotation — from Johann Wolfgang von Goethe — becomes relevant: "There is nothing so terrible as ignorance in action." I suspect
that the human predicament is as much a product of ignorance about
the nature and goals of life, or stupidity in pursuing them, as it is of
cunning, conspiratorial craftiness. And I further suggest that good
people are as much responsible for this ignorance and stupidity as the
bad guys. It is conventional for righteous people to feel that they are
at a disadvantage in most "worldly" contexts because the bad are clev-
erer than they. This may or may not be true, but it is no excuse for
contributing to the kinds of action against which Goethe warned.

How may we as Latter-day Saints effectively implement our
concern for a better world, using the intellectual and spiritual resources
that all have? My hope — and conviction — is that we can accept Burke's
challenge while avoiding Goethe's pitfall.

To expand upon this challenge, I refer to a familiar Persian proverb about ignorance: "He who knows not and knows not that he knows not is a fool; shun him. He who knows not and knows that he knows not is a child; teach him. He who knows and knows not that he knows is asleep; wake him. He who knows and knows that he knows is wise; follow him." I wish to comment briefly on these four combinations of ignorance and knowledge, then add and comment on a fifth type.

As for the person who "knows not and knows not that he knows not," he represents the apathetic masses in most of human history. He made many wise men of the past fearful about democracy, because uninformed people, if somehow provoked to action, often produce Goethe's consequences. The followers in a mob usually come from the ranks of such foolish ones. They know not and know not that they know not until someone proposes a line of action which is intriguing and uncomplicated, which rolls well off the tongue or fits dramatically on a placard or banner.

Another "knows not and knows not that he knows not" manifestation is the sophomore syndrome, in which the possession of vast knowledge is assumed. We have, I trust, passed through that phase, but we should be on guard lest the syndrome reassert itself in later life. The key, of course, is knowing the limits of our knowledge, because all of us "know not" in some areas, and if we "know not that we know not," we may make the mistake of tackling enterprises which had better be left to those with superior skills or information. We ought, as educated people, to know when we need to call in a mechanic, a doctor, a psychiatrist, or a public administrator rather than to seek a solution through intuition or illusions of competency.

The second type in the proverb, who "knows not and knows that he knows not," is the individual with quickening awareness of intellectual possibilities—like Adam or Eve in the Garden of Eden. Formal education has carried us, I hope, beyond the point where we are plastic intellectual material to be molded or written upon. As we face oral or written job-related examinations or questions from teenagers, however, we will find ourselves again in the predicament of knowing that we know not. Good will and steadfastness in seeking knowledge, and modesty in asserting only that knowledge which we truly possess, will help us to deal with the problem of ignorance in ourselves and others.

As for the type who "knows but knows not that he knows," this is a rare phenomenon. So I shall pass it with the observation that those who speak humbly of their knowledge may, in fact, be genuinely modest. On the other hand, to paraphrase Winston Churchill, "They may have a good deal about which to be modest." Humility becomes us all in proper measure.

I turn now to the person who "knows and knows that he knows." He also is rare, but he is a pearl of great price, and the challenge to each of us is to qualify in his own sphere to be such a pearl. One problem is to develop the capacity to recognize those who have effective knowledge in the areas of our weakness, so that we can follow their leadership. An even more formidable responsibility is to recognize when we possess sufficient knowledge so that we are entitled — and obligated — to move out in front and offer leadership for others.

How can we recognize the person with sufficient knowledge to lead? Academic pedigrees are possible clues, but anyone who has been through four years of college should know that you cannot rely on them 100 percent. Practical experience is sometimes a clue; a person who has been involved in the action is likely to have more insight than someone who has viewed from afar. But some people have been trapped in such a rut that their perspective is limited. Office holding, particularly offices of prominence, may entitle persons for respect as possessors of the knowledge which deserves followers, but there are many exceptions. Latter-day Saints have some comfort in the fact that the prophetic office, through which much vital knowledge is transmitted, almost always offers dependable leadership. After all, God knows and knows that he knows; in his counsel we can confidently direct our steps.

As a general response to the Persian proverb, I conclude that we avoid the pitfalls of ignorance by learning for ourselves and by learning how to identify those upon whose knowledge and experience we can rely.

I turn now to another category of ignorance which is, I think, formidable in our world today. Paralleling the proverb, I will characterize it in this language: "He who knows not but knows that he knows is a fanatic; resist him."

The professed knowledge of zealots, crusaders, and leaders of mobs has produced much mischief. Among the murderers of Jesus

Christ, I suggest that those who stood in the crowd shouting, "Crucify him, crucify him," were mostly people who "knew not and knew not that they knew not." It is possible that their leaders "knew and knew that they knew," yet denied their witness of Jesus. But I suspect that they knew not, but were confident that "they knew that they knew" who Jesus was — a heretic and revolutionary who deserved to die.

Two definitions of the term "fanatic" come to mind: "A fanatic is a person who redoubles his efforts after he has lost sight of his goal." Also, "a fanatic is a person who is doing what God would do if God had all the facts."

Of such people another wit once remarked, "It isn't what people don't know that makes the trouble; it's what people know that ain't so."

Professors and promoters of false knowledge are to be found at both ends of any ideological spectrum — in politics, economics, sociology, family-rearing, religion. Push far enough in the direction of commitment to almost any cause and one will find those whose unexpressed slogan is, "My mind is made up; don't confuse me with the facts." Communist and other radical leftist organizations, at one end of the line, are convinced that the American establishment has nothing of salvage value in it, not uncommonly because of unhappy personal experiences or a visceral response to the abundant evil in the world. White supremacists and professional anti-Communists are comparable in temper and often in motivation; they vent their own frustrations on the society whose directions of evolution pose threats to their security and self-image. These are manifestations of ignorance to which, I think, Goethe's statement particularly applies.

There are at least three types of "know not but know that they know" people, or three directions through which people move toward this unhappy and unserviceable condition.

First are the people who are knowledgeable in one area, but who project themselves as authority figures into other areas where their competence is not comparable. Examples are engineers and doctors who know all about Keynes and public finance; child rearing specialists who become experts on national defense; generals who, because they are specialists on "hot" wars, think that they are experts on "cold" wars. Certainly a word of caution is in order against the person who has earned and is entitled to respect in his field but who seeks status and aspires to leadership a long way from his knowledge base.

Second are the people with myopic preoccupations with one area of knowledge, like the blind man who intensively studies the ear of the elephant and offers himself as an authority on elephants. Here are people who produce elaborately footnoted documents to support propositions they knew were true before they began collecting the footnotes from sources which share their predispositions. You can find their hallmarks in the authorized commentaries on the teachings of Chairman Mao and Comrade Lenin, and in books such as *None Dare Call It Treason* and *The Naked Communist*.

A special problem for Latter-day Saints stems, I think, from our confidence that our religion embraces all truth. It leads — or can lead — us to approach all knowledge from a narrow, parochial perspective. I wonder about the confidence with which some of us make sweeping generalizations about what the Catholics believe or what the "religions of the world" believe on the basis of having read nothing more than Mormon publications. Let me make this suggestion about expanding one's knowledge: If everything we read agrees with us, we should enlarge the scope of our reading.

There is a third manifestation of the "knows not-knows-knows" phenomenon, illustrated by an episode that occurred among my colleagues several years ago. We sometimes write memoranda to each other, and if our differences are pronounced, the memos may become at first voluminous and then terse. This particular exchange about a contemporary political question came abruptly to an end when one of the correspondents wrote as his last sentence, "God is my authority, who's yours?"

Because revealed truth is the knowledge upon which Latter-day Saints most confidently rely, and upon which we have a moral obligation to act, it becomes important that our natural yearning for security, for answers, for solutions, does not lead us to project the revelations of God into contexts where they may not apply. Without laboring the point, I suggest that we should all make prayerful private judgment of any dogmatic assertion that "God is my authority" on any question or problem not *clearly*, *categorically*, and *consistently* covered by prophetic teaching.

Assuming that we have resolved with Burke to go into action and with Goethe to avoid the pitfalls of ignorant action, let us take counsel from two passages of scripture. The first is from Doctrine and Covenants 88:118: "Seek ye out of the best books words of wisdom. Seek knowledge by study and also by faith." The second is also from the Doctrine and Covenants. Everyone has responsibilities for action in home, family, church, and vocation which they must not shirk. But as we move daily into a wide and perplexing world — where the challenges are greatest and, in many respects, the knowledge is least secure — let us face it in the spirit of Doctrine and Covenants 58:26-27: "For behold, it is not meet that I should command in all things; for he that is compelled in all things, the same is a slothful and not a wise servant; therefore he receiveth no reward. Verily I say, men should be anxiously engaged in a good cause, and do many things of their own free will, and bring to pass much righteousness; for the power is in them, wherein they are agents unto themselves. And inasmuch as men do good they will in no wise lose their reward."

6

Myths, Documents, and History

THE STUDY OF HISTORY, WHETHER AS PROFESSIONAL OR NON-professional, is fraught with the same perils as the exploration of any field of knowledge — a peril aptly expressed in this slightly paraphrased language of English theologian William Inge: "The fruit of the tree of knowledge always drives us from some Garden of Eden."[1]

I am a Mormon of the Liahona persuasion. I believe in God as the organizer and manager of the eternal enterprise in which we are all engaged. I believe in Jesus Christ as the great exemplar of righteousness and as our redeemer. I believe that we have the right and power to make choices and that the choices make a difference. I believe that Joseph Smith was a prophet and that this church is prophetically led. I do not subscribe to the concepts of scriptural inerrancy or prophetic infallibility. I do believe that God will yet reveal many great and important things pertaining to his work.

As a historian, I accept the challenge of the great nineteenth-century German historian Leopold von Ranke to try to describe the past *wie es eigentlich gewesen ist* — as it actually was. That is a real challenge, and I suspect von Ranke knew that it was only an ideal. It could not be done then and it cannot be done now. Why? Because of the limitations all of us share in approaching any past happening, limitations that no analytical skill or linguistic or statistical tool can transcend. Among these are:

Perspective: Each of us looks at what is happening from a certain point of view; we cannot see it in the round. We have invented machines that do a better job of looking at a thing from all sides than we are able to do with our human perceptions.

Bias: We bring not only a point of view to every event but also prejudices. We may think our approach to books and articles, such as this one, is relatively neutral and dispassionate, but bias — pre-judgment — concerning subject or author had something to do with our decision to read and it will certainly affect what we retain.

Memory: Each of us can remember occasions, either amusing or stressful, in which efforts to recall a relatively recent conversation generated differences about the content and even the conclusions reached. Memory affects all events.

Records: As time and distance affect our memories of an event, we confront our dependence upon documents and artifacts and the problem of the incompleteness and impermanence of all records.

Context: As we try to reconstruct the past, we find that we cannot deal with the whole situation. We look at a happening that has meaning, in part, because of the other things that were going on at the time, but we cannot take them all into account. Some have been forgotten, others have fuzzy details, and the synthesizing of others may be unmanageable.

Selective remembering: We tend to remember some things — like pleasure — better than others — like pain. Sometimes, in looking back, we transform pain into a kind of pleasure, even spiritual exaltation. For example, some of the accounts of the Mormon handcart pioneers give an impression that as their feet froze, they lay in the snowdrifts quietly singing the fourth verse of "Come, Come Ye Saints" while waiting for deliverance.

If all these limitations complicate the historian's reconstruction of a single event, surely he or she should speak of the causes, connections, and meanings of interrelated events and the personalities, ideas, and motives of people with even less certitude, for reasons that readily come to mind. Still, I believe that a competent historian can get close enough to history "as it actually was" to generate provocative, often profitable, sometimes perilous knowledge.

Let me first offer a provocative example that is neither perilous nor particularly profitable.

"The Case of 'This is the Place' " is drawn from my teaching experience. Today's Mormon students say they have grown up with about the same images which I encountered when I first heard about the pioneers over sixty years ago. The Saints were driven out of Nauvoo, Illinois, for a variety of reasons, all classified as "persecution." They were led into an uncharted wilderness by their prophet, Brigham Young. After spending some time there, Brigham, like Moses of old, recognized their destination, rose up in Wilford Woodruff's wagon, and, gazing at the Great Salt Lake Valley, said, "This is the right place. Drive on." They went down into the valley and began to make the desert blossom as the rose.

A problem arises when one discovers that the statement, "This is the right place," was first attributed to Young by Woodruff more than thirty years after the pioneer advent.[2]

That may or may not prove anything. Even what Woodruff wrote at the time may not prove anything, but here is part of his journal entry for 24 July 1847: "This is an important day in the History of my life and the history of the Church. . . . On this important day, after trav[eling] from our encampment 6 miles . . . we came in full view of the great valley or Bason [of] the Salt Lake and land of promise held in reserve by the hand of GOD." He then described the pleasing prospect and reported: "President Young expressed his full satisfaction in the Appearance of the valley as A resting place for the Saints & was Amply repaid for his Journey." Woodruff recorded that they traveled about four miles down to the camp of "our brethren who had arrived two days before. They had . . . broke about five acres of ground and commenced planting potatoes."[3]

It is clear from this contemporary record that, at least in Woodruff's judgment, the hand of the Lord was visible in the selection of the Latter-day Saints' new home. The surprising point is that the memorable Pioneer Day words do not appear in this account. They do turn up in 1880, in a Pioneer Day address given three years after Brigham Young's death. Woodruff was looking back to 1847, and the language nicely epitomizes the sentiments which Young may have expressed, even in those very words. But it is evident that the journal account in some way affects the Pioneer Day tradition, because there were people already down there plowing and planting potatoes by the time Young said, "This is the right place," or whatever it was that he said. Their action obviously had not waited upon this prophetic identification of the spot. That decision had been made earlier as Young considered the options with his colleagues, studied the available geographic information about the Great Salt Lake Valley, and received at least provisional confirmation that this, in God's judgment, *was* the place.

This is no earth-shaking matter, unless it has become important to one that the pioneers did not know where they were going until their leader received a particular miraculous sign. It is simply an illustration of what happens from time to time when memories of the past are tested against contemporary documentation.

It seems fitting to add here that historians, like practitioners of other trades, sometimes speak as one having more authority than they actually do. They are only entitled to dismiss a myth categorically when it alleges that something occurred which, on the basis of evidence, *could not* have occurred. I will give an illustration of this presently. It is entirely competent for someone to argue today that Brigham Young *did* say on the 24th of July, "This is the right place. Drive on." The documents surely suggest that he and others experienced a confirmation of some kind. Only the language is at issue.

However, the number of people who shared that confirmation is not clear from the contemporary evidence. Some who came into the valley in the first few months, including Sam Brannan and some of the Mormon Battalion people who had been to California, thought that perhaps Young ought to ask the question again.

A further caution may be in order here. Historians are not very helpful in determining *how* God communicates with people. They can discover details about the way men and women have said such communication took place and can report and interpret according to their perceptions and biases. They are no better than philosophers, mathematicians, or anybody else in giving definitive answers to the questions which have been vexing people since the first wonderings about where we came from, why we are here, and where we are going.

To return to my theme: Some things in the past are more important than others—more useful than others. We remember them best and we recall them in association with the purpose or cause or value which makes them useful. Sometimes an alteration of the event "as it actually happened" occurs in this process.

This brings us to the term "myth."

Most dictionaries insist that a myth must be fictitious—like a fairy tale. However, that is not what it means to historians. A historical myth is an idealized version of an event which once happened. It is what the memory of an event becomes after people, usually for reasons involving group values, have transformed it so that it is more useful. The process of myth-making distills from the past elements which motivate people to be more patriotic, generous, loving, or virtuous in some other dimension.

This process of taking something out of historic experience and converting it — by addition, subtraction, modification, or revision — into a value-laden symbolic memory can be observed in many contexts. George Washington was hardly dead before the myth-making process began. The cherry tree was added because Parson Weems wanted to make Washington's honesty vivid for children. A Valley Forge prayer which may never have been uttered became one of the most familiar events associated with the father of our country.

Myth making forgets things, too. Sally Fairfax almost disappeared from the Washington record until the diggers into documents and the psycho-historians discovered her again. There was no big scandal here, but there is evidence that Washington, for all his uprightness, never quite got over feeling special about this wife of his good friend, whom he almost certainly would have courted if the friend had not done so first.

We ascribe ideas to people when they have become folk heroes, simply because any cause is strengthened by the support of a mythic figure. I once investigated a quotation on gun control that an op-ed contribution to the *Salt Lake Tribune* (29 Jan. 1984) attributed to George Washington. Here is part of it: "Firearms stand next in importance to the Constitution itself. They are the American people's liberty teeth."

It does not sound like Washington. After going through the index of Washington's collected writings, writing to the Library of Congress legislative reference section and to the author of the *Tribune* article, and finally locating the hate-sheet from which this author obtained the quotation, I am satisfied that Washington never said this. So it belongs, in my opinion, in the five-foot shelf of quotations attributed to people whom we wish very much had said them because they give a little extra cachet to our opinions. The next best thing to having the scriptures to quote is having one of the Founding Fathers or Abraham Lincoln on one's side.

The mythologizing process can be seen in the images which gradually emerge and are accepted as somehow definitive—the pictures of the pilgrims landing on Plymouth Rock or of the sea gulls devouring the crickets in the Great Salt Lake Valley. The statue of Joseph and Emma Smith at the Nauvoo visitors' center is a beautiful idealization of these important people. The statue of Brigham Young on the BYU campus is another. It is fair to say that you may know you have become a myth when you become the subject of a statue. Unless, of course, you are a demagogue who commissions your own statue—a clear sign that you expect to become a myth.

Let us turn next to the tools of the historians.

If an event is in the recent past, historians can use the testimony of witnesses—people who were there or heard about it from people who were there. They also have the artifacts which people leave behind for archaeologists, anthropologists, and antique collectors to find. Mostly, however, historians work with information from documents written on paper, papyrus, wood, metal, stone, or some other material. Only where there are documents can one really begin to "do history."

Putting the bits and pieces together can be exciting, because the evidence sometimes contains surprising things. This is one reason why some people find the work of historians provoking: The surprises we turn up do not always sustain our myths. As with "The Case of 'This Is the Place,'" so with the account which follows.

"The Case of the Missing Convention" involves a myth which is chiefly of interest to historians. It comes out of the Mormon statehood movement of 1849. The key document and the associated problem are described in a brochure, *The State of Deseret*, which Peter Crawley wrote in 1982 to commemorate the acquisition of the two-millionth volume in the Harold B. Lee Library collections at Brigham Young University.

This rare book, *The Constitution of the State of Deseret, together with the journal of the convention which formed it and the proceedings of the legislature consequent thereon*, is a pamphlet of sixteen pages published in September 1849. It gives the text of the constitution and describes the events which produced it and the elections which approved it and selected the first officers for the proposed new Mormon commonwealth in the Great Basin.

Historians for at least two generations have been perplexed by the fact that, according to the available documents, two political activities seemed to be going on simultaneously in early 1849. One — a movement to create a territorial government — produced petitions with several thousand signatures which John M. Bernhisel carried back to Congress. The other — a constitutional convention to create a new state — sent Almon W. Babbitt east to join forces with Bernhisel.[4] Coincident with both, an election in Great Salt Lake City on 12 March 1849 unanimously chose a slate of executive and judicial officers, who began to function immediately. It is not clear from the documents whether those involved saw the proposed political entity as a territory or embryonic state. As Dale Morgan described it, "The Mormons very simply . . . elaborated their ecclesiastical machinery into a political government."[5]

We rationalized away this dissonance or just left it on the back burner until Crawley made some interesting discoveries. Among other things, he found that people who are described in this pamphlet as having attended the March 1849 constitutional convention were doing other things at the time. Further, in the diary of one of the alleged participants he found what the Watergate generation might call "the smoking gun." Here is Franklin D. Richards's entry for Thursday, 19 July, months after some of the events described in the pamphlet were alleged to have occurred: "Attended Council the two weeks past, at which the Memorial[,] Constitution of the State of Deseret, Journal of its Legislature, Bill or Declaration of Rights, and the election of A. W. Babbitt as delegate to Congress, was all accomplished" (Crawley, 9). (Richards was probably referring to the Council of Fifty because no other council was involved with such political matters then.)

Crawley's explanation is persuasive. He notes that the United States had just acquired the Great Basin as part of the spoils of the Mexican War and that national politics was very much in flux before the Compromise of 1850. After the proposal for territorial government was devised and dispatched (and a *de facto* local government was formed), news from the east, including recommendations from Thomas L. Kane, led to the conclusion that statehood should have been sought instead. If California and New Mexico were going for it, why not Deseret? Statehood would give the Mormons the self-government which they really wanted.

However, the decision makers in Great Salt Lake City con-cluded that there was not time to go through the steps of electing, drafting, ratifying, electing again, and then petitioning Congress. They also knew that if they asked for statehood without going through this, they could not succeed. So they created a record. They wrote a con-stitution, borrowing mostly from a copy of Iowa's. They then created minutes and election documents, named members to a legislature, and sent the papers back to Kanesville, Iowa, where Apostle Orson Hyde printed them at the *Frontier Guardian* office because the Salt Lake Val-ley did not yet have an operating press. Babbitt took copies of the pamphlet back to Washington and went to work with Kane and Bernhisel in an unsuccessful effort to secure statehood (Crawley, 10-17).

One can make a credible rationalization for this pamphlet, and Crawley does, but this document is as fraudulent in its content as the Donation of Constantine and the "white salamander letter." It is still precious, but it does raise questions, especially if one has difficulty coping with the fact that an LDS First Presidency created and pub-lished it.

I turn next to a personal episode, "The Case of Elder Poll and the Gift of Tongues." It involves two documents, one contemporary with the event to which the story relates and the other retrospective. In general, a contemporary document is more reliable than a written account produced from memory years after the event. The more that matters involve personal faith and values, the greater the difference in reliability is likely to become.

The first source is my missionary journal. I was a missionary in Bremen, Germany, when war started in 1939. After an unsuccess-ful effort to go to Holland, my companion and I found ourselves in Copenhagen. While it was still thought that some of the missionaries might stay in Scandinavia, Elder Joseph Fielding Smith set me apart to the Danish Mission. I went to the fairy-tale city of Odense to start the second phase of my mission. My linguistic preparation consisted of six weeks in Bremen and two years of college German. In Copenhagen I discovered that there were similarities between the Ger-man and Danish tongues, and I entered hopefully into the task of learn-ing the new language; in Odense, I worked a little harder at it. Within two weeks, however, the decision was made that all the missionaries in Europe were to come home. Of the day that we bade farewell to the Odense Saints, 19 September 1939, here is part of what I wrote:

"Meeting — Relief Society. A pathetic affair. Bro[ther]s Pitcher and Neilson had passed the word around, and everyone was there. And every time the missionaries were mentioned, eyes filled with tears. Bro. H. said we'd probably be expected to say something; so while the lesson was going on, I planned. Came the time, and Bro. H. took charge. He called on Bro. Clark [another one of the "greenies"] and overset [translated] a short . . . swan song for him. . . . after he got through, I talked for a couple of minutes — very slowly — but I believe the Saints were with me [I was talking in Danish]. Afterwards I felt very good when Bro. H. said that I really had the gift of tongues to speak so well after less than two weeks time. I am thankful for whatever is responsible. . . . After the other elders had spoken very sincerely and touchingly, the meeting closed. . . . There followed the ordeal of farewells. Everybody wished 'Gude Rejse,' and it seemed like losing real friends, though I'd known them only such a short time. I labored painfully to converse in Dansk with some of the young folks, and received several compliments on my progress in the language. Such things are a not undesirable supplement to the direct personal joy of achievement."

In 1982 a young man from the Macomb, Illinois, Ward went on a mission to Denmark and was assigned to Odense. While looking through the ward records there, he found an account, written in Danish, with an attached picture of Elder Richard Poll and another missionary, taken on shipboard as they traveled back to the states. I do not know how the picture got there; I suppose the other elder, who had been there longer, sent it back to a friend. This is a translation of that bit of ward history:

"In 1939 Odense received a visit of missionaries on their way home from Germany to the USA. . . . One of them, Elder R. D. Poll, had just arrived in Germany one or two days ago and now was being sent home. During the one and one-half days he was in Denmark he came through Odense and at a church meeting he was asked to speak. He spoke about the rough times that would come, but that people shouldn't fear, but hold fast to the gospel and be faithful to the church and nothing would happen. The strange thing was, he spoke in Danish.

"When the meeting was over, the lady who submitted this article, rushed up to talk to him. She began to talk to him in Danish of course and he looked at her very strangely and soon it was learned he couldn't speak or understand Danish.

"About 20 years later this sister was visiting in America and knew a former Danish missionary who knew Bro. Poll and he told her Bro. Poll was a Professor at BYU. This sister had hundreds of times over the years, thought over that special experience and about convinced herself she must have heard wrong back in 1939, so she went to see him again at his office at BYU. Bro. Poll by now had been in Denmark and could speak some Danish. He confirmed to her that in 1939 he couldn't speak Danish, but remembers very clearly that special meeting where he spoke perfect Danish. As he said to her, 'Such things happen.' "

There is obviously a conflict between the two documents. Not only are there discrepancies in details, but if this sister ever met me in America, the contact was so casual that I have no memory of it. I have no overwhelming urge to write to the bishop of the Odense Ward and tell him to correct the ward history. But what should I do if someone from Odense does come to see me?

Myths abound in our traditionalized church history. The exodus from Nauvoo offers several examples. I was mildly traumatized when, as a young person, I found out that the first refugees did not cross the Mississippi on the ice — the river did not freeze over until two weeks later. Those nine births on Sugar Creek became a perplexing part of the myth when I learned that a few weeks later William Clayton wrote "Come, Come Ye Saints" partly in thanksgiving for the successful arrival of a child to his wife, Diantha, who was still in Nauvoo. Why would nine pregnant women cross the river on that first night if other pregnant women could stay behind? The documents suggest that the untimely births took place when the last group of poor Saints was driven out of Nauvoo in September 1846.

There are problems in other pioneer stories, including the sea gulls and crickets and the traditional account of the calling of the Mormon Battalion. Think of what has happened to the pioneer treks. Although tens of thousands of people came west between 1847 and 1869, the myth-making process has reduced the pioneer experience to Brigham Young's advance company and the handcart pioneers of

1856—neither of them representative. (Young's caravan of 143 men, 3 women, and 2 children was hardly the demographic mix to build up Zion in the Rocky Mountains.) The handcart migration has been reduced to one heroic, tragic episode. Although three thousand people crossed the Great Plains with handcarts between 1856 and 1860, the only ones remembered are the members of the Willie and Martin companies who either did not make it or did so with severe frostbite. The myth invites reflection. Which is the more faith-promoting experience: To cross the plains with nothing more serious than blisters or to leave one's feet along the way?

Many such myths develop to sharpen the focus on cherished values. Folk memory cannot handle eighty thousand or even three thousand people in an interminable series of wagon trains and handcart companies plodding across the plains, so it singles out details most suitable for idealization. This is what we have done with Abraham Lincoln and George Washington and what we do with our own lives. We romanticize some of the events of our youth; we remember them with such vividness now that we can be almost certain that we include details which never happened. We move ourselves closer to the center of the action, accentuating our role. Sometimes we move ourselves in when we were not there at all. It gives us standing with our grandchildren, and it helps our self images.

Incongruities—minor or major disharmonies—abound in our several versions of the past. One may ask, "What difference do they make?" The answer is, "Little, if nothing important is at stake." I suspect that very little depends on whose crops were saved by the sea gulls, or whose great-grandparents suffered with the handcart companies. On the other hand, it may make a great deal of difference if a historical myth has become a significant feature of "some Garden of Eden."

A danger in some historical myths is that by depicting levels of aspiration and accomplishment which transcend the historic events, they lead us to inaccurate assessments of ourselves. The point is often made in talks about the pioneers: "We could never do that." The documents suggest that those people did what they did because they had to do it. We do not know what we would do if we were in their shoes. Some of us might lie down by the path and murmur "and should we die," but I believe most of us would tough it out. People have a capacity to rise to challenges.

If people grow up believing that the heroes and heroines of their past were a different kind of people, without the human traits and vulnerabilities which we have, they have been ill served by their "history." The greater the disparity between myth and event, the greater the potential trauma in confronting the past "as it actually happened." And the more natural the tendency to respond irrationally. Ancient history tells of a soldier who stumbled into town with the report that he was the only survivor of a great battle; he was killed for bringing the bad news.

To recapitulate: Discriminating between myths and documents is important only to historians unless something important to a larger community depends on it. Then the perils of disillusionment arise, and the charges of debunking.

It need not necessarily be so. We had an interesting and encouraging illustration a few years ago of how a document with important implications for institutional traditions and values can be handled. (The fact that the document later turned out to be fraudulent does not, in my opinion, alter the main point.) In 1981 Mark W. Hofmann "found" what purported to be Thomas Bullock's copy of a blessing Joseph Smith, Jr., gave to Joseph Smith III, setting him apart for leadership in the church. Both the Utah Mormons and the Reorganized Latter Day Saints had a stake in this discovery. Its initial impact was to confirm the RLDS position while producing perplexity in the Utah church. How should we handle this in view of what we have been taught?

I happened to be present at the press conference in Salt Lake City where the transfer of the document from our people to the RLDS representatives took place. One of the reporters asked what effect it would have. The spokesmen for both churches said in substance, "It will make very little difference."

That, in fact, is the way it worked out. We Latter-day Saints benefited from the service which one of our younger scholars, D. Michael Quinn, had already rendered in a well-documented article showing that at one time or another, Joseph Smith had considered several alternative ways of handling the succession. The Joseph Smith III blessing document fitted very comfortably into that context of alternatives.[6] The issue was handled well because the worth of neither church depended on that document, nor did the testimonies of their members.

How well—how righteously—life is lived does not depend on either myths or documents about the past. The myth-making process contributes to the pursuit of righteousness to the extent that it provides ideal models and motivating traditions which are consistent with truth. The historians with their documents contribute to the pursuit of righteousness to the extent that they check the myth-making capability to generate and perpetuate untruths and half-truths and even to sanctify unrighteousness.

Only God knows the past "as it actually happened." Whether we are myth-makers or myth-shakers, we see history "through a glass darkly." Properly understood, both myths and documents can assist our quest for that understanding of yesterday which can be helpful in coping with today and making choices for tomorrow.

— *Notes* —

1. The exact quotation, as it appears without source citation in class notes my wife, Gene, and I took when we audited P. A. Christensen's BYU course on Milton, is: "The fruit of the tree of knowledge always drives man from some Paradise or other; and even the Paradise of fools is not an unpleasant abode while it is habitable."

2. *Utah Pioneers* (Salt Lake City, 1880), 23, quoted in Leland H. Creer, *The Founding of an Empire* (Salt Lake City, 1947), 302n93.

3. Scott G. Kenney, ed., *Wilford Woodruff's Journal* (Salt Lake City: Signature Books, 1983), 3:233-34.

4. Dale L. Morgan, "The State of Deseret," *Utah Historical Quarterly* 8 (April, July, and Oct. 1940), 2-4:67-155. Most subsequent treatments of this subject have been based on this monograph. It was reprinted in 1987 by the Utah State University Press.

5. Morgan, 34. It does not appear from Morgan or Crawley that the name State of Deseret was used before the makers of the proposed state constitution adopted this name in the state-making events described by Crawley.

6. D. Michael Quinn, "The Mormon Succession Crisis of 1844," *Brigham Young University Studies* 16 (Winter 1976), 2:187-233.

7

Our Changing Church

In October 1984, Elder Ronald E. Poelman, a member of the LDS church's First Quorum of the Seventy, spoke on "The Gospel and the Church." Several sentences from that address express the concept that underlies this essay (what eventually happened to the address is described in a later essay):

"Both the Gospel of Jesus Christ and the Church of Jesus Christ are true and divine. However, there is a distinction between them and it is very important that this distinction be understood. . . . The Gospel is the substance of the divine plan for personal, individual salvation and exaltation. The Church is the delivery system that provides the means and resources to implement this plan in each individual's life. . . . In the scriptures we discover that varying institutional forms procedures, regulations, and ceremonies are utilized, all divinely designed to implement eternal principles. The practices and procedures change; the principles do not."

The Church of Jesus Christ of Latter-day Saints, which is my subject here, is an institution of this world, at least in the sense that it will be radically different in structure, programs, and membership when it is transplanted into the next world. The church is to serve us in the here and now.

As a student and observer of human experience, I suggest that in this world institutions have two options. They either change or they die. They become obsolete and disappear, as did the Roman empire, or they show sufficient flexibility to accommodate a chang-

73

ing context and so remain vigorous, as has the government of the United States — so far.

We Latter-day Saints have a tendency, in dealing with our own relatively short history, to telescope it into a shorter time span than it has actually occupied and to overlook the changes that have occurred. The president of the United States at the time of Joseph Smith's first vision was James Monroe, only the fifth man to hold that office and one of the founding fathers. John Adams and Thomas Jefferson were still alive and writing to each other. The Monroe Doctrine came three years later, about the time of the Angel Moroni's first visitation to Joseph Smith. As much time has elapsed from then to now as had elapsed going backward from then to the days of the Salem witch trials. The tempo of changes has been much more rapid, and the context of life has changed much more radically in the last one hundred and fifty-odd years than in any period of similar length since historical annals began. A great historian once said that George Washington, if he were to come back in the twentieth century, would feel more a stranger than if he returned to the time of the Egyptian pharaohs. The work of the Restoration has been carried forward in a changing world.

One of the interesting things about the process of historical myth-making is that it tends to lift an institution out of its context. Everybody who is into Mormon history knows how U.S. president Martin Van Buren turned the prophet Joseph Smith aside, saying something that led him to be remembered as an enemy of the Saints. But some of us would be hard-pressed to remember anything else about President Van Buren. It is the same way with Senator Stephen A. Douglas. All we know about him is that he failed to become president of the United States because of a prophecy that Joseph Smith is said to have spoken about him. We are oddly ambiguous about Abraham Lincoln, because he has his own set of good myths and we modern Mormons no longer see the United States as an enemy of the Kingdom of God. So we have forgotten that Lincoln ran on a Republican platform which attacked polygamy, that he baited Stephen A. Douglas for being soft on the Mormons, and that he signed the first anti-polygamy act passed by Congress. We have selective memories about our heroes in both our political and ecclesiastical traditions.

An interesting illustration of this tendency is being explored by Carma DeJong Anderson, an authority on the history of clothing and fashions. She argues persuasively that we have clothed all the historic figures of the founding generation of the Mormon church in the wrong kinds of clothes — styles which were not worn in their period of time. (The clothes are never dirty either, even in representations of Liberty Jail.) It is unlikely that anyone living or dead will be upset by this disclosure, but the little things add up to big things and the big things may become important. We do not want to get to the point where something important depends upon whether Joseph Smith wore a certain kind of suit when he did this or that as a New York farm boy or as mayor of Nauvoo, Illinois.

Context affects all kinds of institutions in this world, including churches. Persecution produces one institutional reaction; acceptance produces another. Hard times produce one set of challenges; prosperity another. War and peace have their effects, as do changes in demographics and in technology. Diverse cultural environments obviously affect institutions, and one of the exciting things to observe now is how becoming a worldwide church is influencing many aspects of our ecclesiastical organization and the way we approach our mission.

My thesis is that this church has changed significantly as it has pursued its mission in a changing world. I will illustrate the thesis with specific cases, some trivial and some substantial. I will comment in some cases on the causes which may have given rise to the changes, but I am primarily concerned that we simply reaffirm, or discover, that changes *have* occurred. I will then draw one or two general conclusions.

For much of what follows, I acknowledge my indebtedness to the most useful single volume of Mormon history to appear in the last half-century, James B. Allen's and Glen M. Leonard's *The Story of the Latter-day Saints* (Salt Lake City: Deseret Book, 1976). It is valuable for at least three reasons: it is a comprehensive and well proportioned survey of developments from the days of Joseph Smith and Brigham Young down to our own day; it places these developments in a larger context, so that the reader is aware of circumstances and events that impinged upon the church at the time new revelations were received and changes occurred; and it has a very extensive and useful bibliography.[1]

Let us first note some changes in visible externals, including the name of the church itself. It has been The Church of Jesus Christ of Latter-day Saints for so long that some of us have forgotten it was first the Church of Christ, then the Church of Jesus Christ, and then, for a while, the Church of the Latter Day Saints. Not until an 1838 revelation was the name adopted which has become part of our institution (Allen and Leonard, 47). An interesting bit of trivia is that the Utah church uses the form "Latter-day Saints," while the RLDS church uses a capital "D" and no hyphen, "Latter Day Saints." I have no idea how the difference developed, but I do know that it is important to observe the customs of each culture in this matter.

The nature of the buildings in which we gather to worship has, of course, changed over the years. Who is old enough to remember "cry rooms"? Boy Scout rooms? Relief Society rooms that were for Relief Society only? Who remembers bishops' storehouses and tithing offices? The conversion of tithes and offerings from in-kind to cash made most of these ward and stake storage facilities obsolete. Our children will be unable to remember when stake centers lacked satellite dishes, and some of them may imagine that Book of Mormon King Benjamin's sermon was transmitted by such devices.

In the days of Joseph Smith there were no meeting houses; the Saints usually met in homes. Sometimes they gathered in other people's churches, if they could get permission, and sometimes they converted whole congregations in the process. They met in the open air when weather permitted, and when the first temples were completed, they sometimes met there. The plan of Joseph Smith's City of Zion shows twenty-four temples, which would suggest many functions other than those we now specifically associate with temples. Some of the most interesting meetings in Nauvoo were on the second floor of the prophet's store; there the first Relief Society meetings were held and the first temple endowments were performed. In the Brigham Young era the Saints met in boweries made of brush and other natural materials and in tabernacles. They built meeting houses which were also schools and community centers, and of course they built temples, too.

The Latter-day Saints have generally been practical in architecture. Form has followed function. There was a time when one feature of meeting houses was so conspicuous that a non-Mormon visitor asked if basketball was a part of the Mormon religion. The ward library has become a more important feature in the last few years, and that is a heartening trend. Changes in temple design and size have been apparent to all whose first recommends were received a generation or more ago.[2]

A change in doctrinal emphasis is relevant to the changed attitude toward physical facilities. The failure to build meeting houses in the early days reflected the poverty of the Saints, but it also reflected their immediate expectation of the Millennium. When I helped build a chapel in Macomb, Illinois, the contractor said he had never seen such specifications; it looked like the building was meant to last for eternity. I pointed out that that was the idea.

Church publications have changed in amazing ways. The early generations produced doctrinally-oriented tracts with names such as *A Voice of Warning* and *Rays of Living Light*. People were converted on the basis of reading the closely reasoned and scripture-based arguments set forth. Now the tracts are largely public relations pieces meant to persuade readers that they ought to contact the missionaries or otherwise expose themselves to the conversion opportunity. The style has changed; even the packaging of Joseph Smith's own story has evolved over the years.

As for newspapers, it is a long evolution from *The Evening and Morning Star* and *The Times and Seasons* to the *Deseret News*. Magazines have come and gone, too. The first were published in the missions and by the auxiliary organizations. It was a sad milestone, at least from the historian's point of view, when the *Millennial Star* died not too many years ago after having been published for over a century — the longest continuous publication of the church. Once LDS women had their own magazines — *The Women's Exponent* and *The Relief Society Magazine*. Now we have magazines oriented to age groups, not to the sexes or particular programs. The best media technology and talent are now brought to bear. The computer in the clerk's office, like the meeting-house TV set and VCR, are recent signs that in the communications and public relations fields, the church "has come a long way."

For a long time the Tabernacle Choir was almost the only public relations asset that the church had. In the last three decades visitors' centers at historic sites and world fairs, advertisements in *Readers Digest*, television spots, and other promotional techniques have been employed to produce a favorable disposition toward the Mormons and their religion.[3]

The eternal principle of priesthood is that God delegates authority to act in his name. Changes in the institutional expression of that concept are well-documented and continuing. Most of us are familiar with the development of priesthood organization in the days of the prophet Joseph, when new offices and quorums appeared as church growth occurred and experience showed what worked and what did not work so well. Some of these early institutions are still undergoing significant change. The offices of regional representative and area president have appeared within the last generation, for example, while the calling of assistant to the Quorum of the Twelve Apostles has come and gone and the office of Patriarch to the Church, once held by Joseph Smith, Sr., and Hyrum Smith, has disappeared.

A few years ago members interested in church history were excited by the rediscovery of a leadership agency which had disappeared from our collective memory. The Council of Fifty was organized in Nauvoo at a time when the prophet anticipated the early establishment of what was then called the Kingdom of God. The kingdom was not then conceived in the spiritual or other-worldly terms which we talk about now; it was to be a community of Saints standing alone in this world, and it was coming *soon*. The Council of Fifty was to plan for this kingdom and in time to legislate for it. It was a secular, political, this world-oriented planning group. Non-Mormons who were sympathetic to the church might be invited to participate; Daniel H. Wells joined the council before he joined the church and went on to become one of Brigham Young's counselors.

Joseph Smith died before the mission of the Council of Fifty had been very clearly defined; what it might have become had he lived is impossible to say. During the apostolic interregnum and first years of Young's presidency the council handled some of the secular business of the church, but it gradually declined for want of a primary function. The Council of the Twelve and other ecclesiastical bodies did the work. President John Taylor made an effort to revive the Council of Fifty in the 1880s, but if it did anything then or thereafter, those doings are not publicly documented. As far as I know, it is only a historic phenomenon now.[4]

Within the Melchizedek priesthood, nothing has changed more than the calling and organization of the seventy. The first quorum of seventies with its seven presidents was formed in the Kirtland era to provide missionary support to the Quorum of the Twelve and the standing high councils (D&C 107:25-26, 34, 93-97; 124:138-39). Several additional quorums followed. Then, in connection with the movement to Utah and subsequent organizational developments there, the first quorum lost membership and the seven presidents were co-opted into the leadership group. They became General Authorities, and the rest of the quorum was left unmanned. After the thirty-five-year experiment with the assistants to the Quorum of the Twelve, it was decided in the 1970s to revive the First Quorum of the Seventy and make it the center of bureaucratic leadership for the church. The titles "executive director" and "managing director," carried by so many of the members of this quorum, are suggestive. The recently implemented policies of emeritus status and rotation in office and the newly created Second Quorum of the Seventy further suggest that these quorums have become a pool of experienced and dedicated managerial people to help a worldwide and multi-million-member community of believers move forward.

Parallel developments have affected the priesthood office of seventy itself. B. H. Roberts, one of the presidents of the First Quorum of the Seventy in the Joseph F. Smith/Heber J. Grant era, argued persistently that the seventies under the direction of his quorum should have the primary missionary responsibility. What has unfolded is not what Roberts had in mind at all. One interesting aspect of the First and Second Quorums is that their members are all ordained high priests as well as seventies, because some of the assignments which must be performed at that level of church administration require the authority of a high priest. Decades ago the practice of ordaining young male missionaries as seventies began to be discontinued. Now, with the 1986 dissolution of all quorums of seventy except these two nontraditional bodies, it appears that the office of seventy as a separate priesthood calling will eventually disappear.[5]

The Aaronic priesthood has also undergone significant developments. Priests, teachers, and deacons were adults in the early days of the church. Sometime after the Saints came West, the ordination of young men to these offices began, the rationale being that it would involve the youth in church activity and help to make them readier for missions. Teachers, who in the early days had been given an adult responsibility to straighten up the Saints, now were young men without the same competencies for the task. What happened to the home teaching program then? Mormons who have been around for a long time know that there has been an ongoing search for the best way to make a program, superb in concept, work with teaching pairs who are often unequally yoked together. When holders of the Melchizedek priesthood were first called to go with the Aaronic priesthood teachers, they were called "acting teachers" and were set apart for that function. Now, of course, the whole body of the priesthood has been involved in home teaching, and the program bears the onus of a law of institutional dynamics — few people assign high priority to work which is everybody's responsibility. The recent authorization of home teaching by married couples — an approach considered by the hierarchy and rejected a generation ago — shows that the search goes on.

There have been other changes in priesthood quorum functions. Under Joseph Smith, quorums developed in the various centers of activity following revelations which responded to institutional needs. In the tough business of settling the West, the quorums tended to be used, to the extent that they were used at all, on an *ad hoc* basis for getting specific jobs done. (A parallel would be the way the priesthood organizations were used for spring flood fighting in 1983.) What actually happened was a rather serious deterioration in quorum organization and activity in the early Utah days. One of the notable but hardly remembered highlights of Brigham Young's ministry was the wholesale reorganization of priesthood quorums and programs which he initiated just before his death in 1877.[6] With regular meetings came a need for priesthood instruction; B. H. Roberts wrote a great course of lessons for the seventies, and others wrote good lessons for various constituencies. Then began the quest for the best times to meet. Anybody as old as I am can remember when high priests met on week nights, Sunday mornings, or Sunday afternoons, always in competition with the activities of the church auxiliaries.

Only in the last twenty-five years has there been, in the Correlation Program, an effort to put the priesthood back into the center of things and to train and motivate its holders to fulfill the mission defined in the principle. The impact of this effort on institutional procedures, relations between the sexes, and the content and thrust of church educational programs is still being felt.

We have been a "gathering" people from the beginning, but the pattern of congregational structuring has changed significantly. Stakes came and went during the early years. At the time Brigham

Young instituted the priesthood reforms of 1877, there were eight stakes in the whole church; Salt Lake Valley was one stake. As far as organized missions were concerned, the only permanent mission installation was in Liverpool, England. It published *The Millennial Star*, coordinated the activities of the European missions, and was the funnel through which the gathering to Zion moved.

In the 1877 reform the apostles, some of whom had been running church affairs in various locations — for example, Erastus Snow in southern Utah, Lorenzo Snow in Brigham City, and Charles C. Rich in Cache Valley — were called back to participate in overall church management. Stake presidencies were organized and the number of stakes was increased immediately to eighteen. The stake presidents were given counselors and were instructed to hold quarterly conferences, submit reports, and more systematically supervise the wards and branches within their jurisdictions.

This pattern of gradually developing new stakes according to need and holding quarterly conferences in conjunction with apostolic visits continued to my day. Since the David O. McKay era the trend has accelerated; more and more stakes have been created and smaller stakes have become the norm. The first overseas stake came in 1959, 129 years after the church was organized. A century before, when there were more Latter-day Saints in England than in Utah, there was no overseas stake organization because gathering to America was the thing to be done. Now there are stakes almost everywhere there are missions, and most of the missionary activity is within the boundaries of stakes.

The wards have also changed radically. There were no wards until the Nauvoo period, when the first were formed primarily as units of economic management. The bishop was assigned to look after the poor and take care of certain secular functions, a pattern which continued under Brigham Young in Utah. The bishop was the man through whom instructions might be sent to call for men, wagons, and livestock to meet the annual immigration. He was the man who collected tithing, dispensed some of it locally, and sent the rest through one of the traveling bishops into the Salt Lake City tithing center. The job was demanding at times but not as demanding in terms of total time commitment as the calling of bishop is now. Bishops then served for years and years, sometimes dying in office. The same was true of stake presidents.

In the 1877 reforms, the office of bishop was institutionalized, with two counselors who were to be high priests. That pattern continued until recent times. Then it was discovered that student wards at BYU and other universities were flooding the church with very young high priests, who had become members of bishoprics in campus communities. So policies were modified to permit a bishop to have non-high priests as counselors in such non-typical wards.

In response to changing circumstances the pattern of ward meetings has also changed. Latter-day Saints were not so habituated to meetings in the founding generations as we have since become. Meetings were less frequent, but they were also long, as reports of sermons in the *Messenger and Advocate*, *The Evening and the Mormon Star*, and Joseph Smith's history disclose. One of the amusing things about Wilford Woodruff's diary is that he reports how many minutes everybody spoke at almost every meeting he attended for a period of about sixty years. To add up some of those numbers is to become aware that meetings in those days were regarded not only as instructional and inspirational but also as a form of recreation for those who chose to attend.

In my youth, participation in sacrament meetings was just beginning to be stressed, and a 25 percent attendance rate was phenomenal. As the meetings became more important, there was a period within recent memory when it was not a proper sacrament meeting unless it went for an hour and a half. Now if it goes more than an hour and ten minutes, a lot of Sunday school teachers become nervous. The three-hour block schedule is one of those innovations responsive to changing circumstances which one can easily identify, and its own problems are already becoming apparent.

With fair frequency, possible solutions to problems are tested through pilot programs in one or more localities. It was so with the block plan for meetings, and it is likely to be so with whatever meeting arrangement supplants it. Without special insight or authority, I suggest that the next format for meetings may incorporate a sacrament meeting and a Sunday school (with opening exercises), separated by an interval long enough to permit some social visiting and the transaction of some person-to-person business; Relief Society and priesthood quorum business meetings will supplant Sunday school lessons once a month, but gender-segregated courses of instruction will disappear.

A generation ago many sacrament meetings featured itiner-
ant preachers who were invited to ward after ward because they gave
unusually interesting talks. Every once in a while a charismatic convert got on the circuit, became a cult figure, and then disappeared
without a trace. Now almost all sacrament meeting programs are home-
grown, and fully developed gospel sermons are almost as rare as
appearances by "celebrities" and testimonies in tongues.

Even the criteria for fellowshipping have changed. In the nineteenth century the Word of Wisdom received much less emphasis, particularly in its tea and coffee dimensions. Only within my lifetime has
full compliance become a requirement for holding offices and callings in the church. On the other hand, under Joseph Smith and
Brigham Young some Mormons were excommunicated for attending
non-Mormon dances, failing to accept mission calls, using tobacco
and intoxicants, gossiping, failing to tithe, Sabbath-breaking, patron-
izing non-Mormon businesses, and failing to follow counsel. At the
same time rebaptism was readily available, not only for readmission
to the church but as a token of repentance and rededication for members in good standing.

The proselyting program is another good example of opera-
tional changes to serve enduring principles. In the early days missionary work was epitomized by the phrase "without purse or scrip." Missionaries went out, often leaving families behind, and some of the
ways they survived seem marvelous, even miraculous. Theirs was an
individual enterprise. They wrote their own tracts and letters to edi-
tors. Once they made converts to the idea that the gospel had been
restored, they preached the doctrine of gathering, which retained a
powerfrul appeal for converts until the end of the nineteenth century.
Echoes of it were still heard in the mission field in the 1930s, when I
was at work in Germany, Denmark, and Canada.

Around the turn of the century, the missionary program
evolved away from calling husbands to leave their families and into
the pattern of calling young unmarried men and some young single
women. The missionary environment became somewhat more structured, but what actually happened depended on the temperament and
leadership style of the mission president and the motivation and temperament of the individual missionary. At a recent reunion of Canadian missionaries of the David A. Smith era, 1939-43, we agreed that

it had not been the best period of missionary work, if one thought in terms of "the field is white, ready for the harvest." I baptized one young man in my two years; some others did better and some did worse.

Since World War II there have been significant changes in the missionary program. The idea that missionaries might do better if they had some formal instruction and a plan to follow gave rise to an elaborate and now world-wide training program. A structured proselyting plan was given churchwide application in 1961; it has undergone several modifications since. Building missionaries, health missionaries, and school teachers have performed specialized functions under church calls. Missionaries from the mission fields have now ended what was for a century a virtual monopoly of Saints from the American West. More recently, the use of senior people has opened a tremendous manpower — and womanpower — pool. President McKay's dictum, "Every member a missionary," gave this aspect of Mormonism a thrust which President Kimball's "Lengthen your stride" reinforced.

Church programs for women have also changed. The special role of women was recognized in the founding of the first Relief Society and in the definition and the content of some of the sacred ordinances of the Nauvoo period. Historians, some of them not surprisingly women, are finding much evidence in diaries and other documents that their female progenitors enjoyed helping with these ordinances, anointing and blessing one another, speaking in tongues, and doing other things which manifested the presence of the Holy Spirit.

The Relief Society fell into disorganization during the move west and then was revived as a service organization, with assignments including moral and economic retrenchment, producing silk, defending plural marriage, and promoting women's suffrage. Particularly under the vigorous leadership of Eliza R. Snow and her immediate successors, the Relief Society had a broad influence on the cultural and community life of Utah. Then, as the church began to be transformed from an organized community into a religious institution, the roles of women changed. The autonomy of their organizations was curtailed. They were specifically instructed in 1914 to desist from anointing and blessing one another or their children. World War I saw the disposing of the Relief Society wheat supply, and later the funds accumulated from that enterprise were merged with the general funds of the church. The *Relief Society Magazine* is something remembered with affection now that it is gone.[7]

Both the women's movement and the entry of LDS women into the work force are modifying rank-and-file commitment to the Victorian middle-class family model as the only gospel standard; the growth of the church worldwide is apparently reinforcing this trend. But the dedication to church service remains strong. "Were they but given the opportunity," a prominent female historian recently said of her Mormon sisters, "[women might] take over." Viewed in the context of the movement for women's rights, the Priesthood Correlation Program of the past generation might be seen as an effort to protect the church against that possibility.

A major organizational development of the twentieth century, and particularly the last generation, has been the bureaucratization of the church. I do not use the term in a pejorative sense. Any organization that grows beyond a certain size is bound to develop a bureaucratic structure. From the directors of headquarters divisions and the area presidencies to the property managers and educational supervisors in the missions, more and more professional people are conducting various activities of the church. There may still be no "paid ministry," but the church civil servants receive almost competitive salaries and the leaders who minister full time are compensated according to their needs. The skyscraper at 50 East North Temple Street symbolizes the administrative requirements of growth. If Joseph Smith were to drop in on the Monday morning staff meeting of almost any department in the church tower, I wonder what he would say.

So many changes! Whatever happened to the M Men and Gleaner Girls? Who can remember the common sacrament cup? Or the time when priests, in blessing the sacrament, raised their right arms to the square and the deacons, in passing the emblems, put their left hands behind them? When taking the sacrament with the wrong hand was an offense comparable in moral significance to using "you" instead of "thou" in prayer? So many things remind us that "The old order changeth, yielding place to the new, and God fulfills himself in many ways."

The time to prepare children to cope with institutional changes is when you are trying to explain what happened to Santa Claus, or "You Who Unto Jesus," or Daddy's seventies quorum. I do believe in giving milk before meat, but I do not think children should be taught *anything*, the *unlearning* of which will be traumatic. If we create in them the impression that the church does not change, or that only trivial things change, we create a risk, because some changes are substantial. One valuable consequence of believing in a living prophet — as child or adult member — is that the concept legitimizes change, not only by addition, but by deletion and modification. Even simple faith can cope with the idea that some institutional policies and practices are abandoned because they are outgrown and others because they simply do not work out as planned.

The student who looks at LDS history finds everywhere confirmation of Elder Poelman's distinction between eternal principles, which are accessible through the eye of faith, and changing institutions, which may be studied through documents and other tools of the historian's craft. Given what history and other disciplines tell us about institutional dynamics, the current vigor of the church is *prima facie* evidence that it has changed since the 1830s. Finally, in the perspective of the Ninth Article of Faith, past changes should not surprise us, nor should the virtual certainty of future changes cause distress.

— Notes —

1. A revised and updated edition of *The Story of the Latter-day Saints* is now in preparation. Leonard J. Arrington and Davis Bitton, *The Mormon Experience* (New York: Alfred A. Knopf, 1979), is another useful survey, written primarily for a non-LDS audience.

2. This is probably not the place to discuss the ordinances and practices associated with the temple, but they have not been immune to change. See David John Buerger, "The Development of the Mormon Temple Endowment Ceremony," *Dialogue: A Journal of Mormon Thought* 20 (Winter 1987), 4:33-76; Buerger, " 'The Fullness of the Priesthood': The Second Anointing in Latter-day Saint Theology and Practice," *Dialogue* 16 (Spring 1983), 1:10-44; and D. Michael Quinn, "Latter-day Saints Prayer Circles," *Brigham Young University Studies* 19 (Fall 1978), 4:79-105.

3. One of Mormon humorist Calvin Grondahl's cartoon books which makes friendly fun of Mormon folkways carries the title *Marketing Precedes the Miracle* (Salt Lake City: Signature Books, 1987).

4. See Klaus J. Hansen, *Quest for Empire: The Political Kingdom of God and the Council of Fifty in Mormon History* (East Lansing: Michigan State University Press, 1967).

5. It is interesting that the principle of common consent was not invoked to sustain the abandonment of the priesthood offices of seventy or church patriarch. The curtailment of the traditional voting by priesthood quorums when Ezra Taft Benson was sustained as president of the church may be another evidence of how the concept of common consent has over time been transformed from a substantive procedure to a ceremonial rite.

6. William G. Hartley, "The Priesthood Reorganization of 1877: Brigham Young's Last Achievement," *Brigham Young University Studies* 20 (Fall 1979), 1:3-36.

7. See Maureen Ursenbach Beecher and Lavina Fielding Anderson, eds., *Sisters in Spirit: Mormon Women in Historical and Cultural Perspective* (Urbana: University of Illinois Press, 1987); Claudia L. Bushman, ed., *Mormon Sisters: Women in Early Utah* (Cambridge, MA: Emmeline Press, 1976); and Vicky Burgess-Olson, ed., *Sister Saints* (Provo: Brigham Young University Press, 1978).

8

Confronting the Skeletons

A CHARACTERISTIC OF ALMOST ANY INSTITUTION'S HANDLING OF
its experience and traditions is the effort to sanitize certain aspects of
its history. We tidy up the record. We put shiny new shoes on feet of
clay and fashionable clothes upon skeletons which will not stay forgotten in the closet of the past.

We Latter-day Saints do so in interesting ways. I have never
seen a pictorial representation of the first vision in which Joseph Smith
was wearing a frayed or dirty shirt, in which he had uncombed hair,
or in which there was dirt on his bare feet. I am mildly intrigued by
the fact that, despite our doctrinal understanding that the suffering of
the Savior in the Garden of Gethsemane caused him to bleed pro-
fusely, no pictures of scenes associated with the betrayal show his
garments stained with blood. These trivial details—white and clean
images—illustrate what we commonly do in the process of represent-
ing ideally the things which are important to us.

These are small matters, easy to dismiss. However, when we
deal with embarrassing or difficult episodes, the sanitizing takes on
more significance, especially if people begin depending on the sani-
tized version to protect their values and commitments.

Two illustrations of the sanitizing process in Mormon history are the traditional treatments of the Mountain Meadows Massacre and of plural marriage.

The Mountain Meadows Massacre is difficult to idealize. The
most utilitarian approach, institutionally speaking, is to forget about

it, and the Mormon people have tried hard to do so. In recent times, historians with their musty documents — primarily a historian named Juanita Brooks — have helped us to confront an embarrassing, tragic episode in our collective past. The process has been beneficial.

The Mountain Meadows Massacre occurred in southwestern Utah, west of Cedar City on 11 September 1857. The Fancher party, about 137 California-bound immigrants (mostly from Arkansas, some from Missouri), were attacked by a group of white settlers and Indians in such a fashion that only seventeen young children survived. Units of the local militia were involved along with Paiute Indians more or less indigenous to the area. The whites were Latter-day Saints.

A myth quickly developed, for obvious reasons. It went so far in the direction of falsehood that in 1890, when Hubert Howe Bancroft published his *History of Utah* (San Francisco: The History Company, 1890), relying almost exclusively on Utah Mormon sources, he wrote: "This horrible crime . . . was the crime of an individual, the crime of a fanatic of the worst stamp, one who was a member of the 'Mormon Church,' but of whose intentions the Church knew nothing, and whose bloody acts, the members of the Church, high and low, regard with as much abhorrence as any out of the Church" (p. 544).

The course of myth development had by then placed the blame for this tragic action upon one man, John D. Lee, whom I learned as a boy to regard as a renegade. I knew nothing else about him except that ultimately he paid with his life for his crime.

What changed in the half-century after Bancroft? Very little. Many editions of Joseph Fielding Smith's *Essentials in Church History* (Salt Lake City: Deseret Book Company, 1950) expressed the institutional version of the crime. This is the way it stood when I began teaching history at BYU: "It was the deed of enraged Indians aided by a number of white men, who took vengeance into their hands for wrongs committed by a few of the emigrants who were pronounced enemies of both whites and Indians. . . . For several years the facts relating to the tragedy were unknown, but gradually the truth leaked out and an investigation was made of the affair. John D. Lee was excommunicated from the Church with the injunction from President Young that under no circumstances should he ever be admitted as a member again. Action was also taken against others as the truth became known. In later years Lee was convicted of the crime and paid the penalty with his life. . . . Others who were implicated fled from the territory and died fugitives. While they thus evaded the justice which earthly tribunals might inflict, they still await the trial for their crimes before a Higher Court where justice never fails" (pp. 510, 516-17). Lee is the only individual named in this account.

It is now clear that institutional self-interest had created a scapegoat and minimized the entire affair. The horror of Mountain Meadows had been hidden in a myth-closet, as family skeletons are often concealed.

How does one recover this bit of the past "as it really happened"? Juanita Brooks showed how in her book, *The Mountain Meadows Massacre*, which came out in 1950 from Stanford University Press and in 1962 in a revised edition from the University of Oklahoma Press. It is still the primary reference.

Brooks's documentation is a fine example of historical detective work. She went to the records of people who were around at the time, insofar as they could be found. One can understand that those directly involved did not write extensive memoirs. Helpful on many topics and particularly on this are the diaries of John D. Lee, which Brooks found and published. The first of the two published volumes provides some circumstantial evidence, but the events at Mountain Meadows are not recorded. Later, under the impetus of a feeling of betrayal and the immediate prospect of execution, Lee described the event in a confessional volume which is also helpful. Using these and other sources listed in her extensive bibliographies, Brooks wrote a full-length biography of Lee, *John Doyle Lee: Zealot, Pioneer Builder, Scapegoat* (Glendale: The Arthur H. Clark Company, 1962), which establishes that he was not "a fanatic of the worst stamp" but an important builder of pioneer Utah.

In looking at what happened from a historian's perspective, I acknowledge my indebtedness to Juanita Brooks, whom I heard describe the massacre at the site some years ago. What she did, and what I think the historical reconstruction of any mythologized past event should do, is to help us see more accurately *what* happened and even more importantly to help us understand *why*.

We are dealing with people like ourselves, people who do not change very much from one generation to another in terms of capacity to be excited, to be depressed, to become fighting mad, or to rise to heroic achievements. The Mormons of southern Utah in 1857 were as capable as we of high aspirations and abysmal shortfalls.

One of the background factors which helps to explain the massacre is the strong millennialism then influencing the Latter-day Saints. They felt that the time was *very* short, that the prophesied apocalypse was very near, and that the forces of God and the forces of evil were locked in combat. This expectation tended to convert many worldly contacts into "we-they" confrontations.

A second factor is the early Mormon response to persecution—of which there had been plenty, some brutal. Most of it was no more justified than other instances of religious persecution, past or present. The LDS response was not, in every instance, to follow the admonition, "If a man smite thee on one cheek, turn to him the other also." A remarkable expression of the contrary reaction is found in Sidney Rigdon's famous 4th of July sermon, delivered shortly before the Saints were driven from Missouri under an exterminating order from the governor of the state. At the time Rigdon was a counselor in the First Presidency. Here is Rigdon's language: "But from this day and this hour we will suffer it no more. We take God and all the holy angels to witness, this day, that we warn all men, in the name of Jesus Christ to come on us no more for ever, for from this hour we will bear it no more; our rights shall no more be trampled on with impunity; *the man, or the set of men who attempt it, do it at the expense of their lives. And that mob that comes on us to disturb us, it shall be between us and them a war of extermination; for we will follow them until the last drop of their blood is spilled; or else they will have to exterminate us, for we will carry the seat of war to their own houses and their own families and one party or the other shall be utterly destroyed.*"[1]

It is arguable, and church historian B. H. Roberts does so, that Rigdon's rhetoric got the best of him. One thing which historians learn, however, is that people act upon what they *believe* to be the case, not upon what a calm, clinical after-the-fact analysis shows the case to be. As in Missouri, so in southern Utah nineteen years later, some Latter-day Saints responded to provocation in ways less than praiseworthy.[2]

Another factor operating in 1857 was the recent Mormon Reformation, a time of revitalization in which the Saints had been called to recommit to their covenants and had been reminded of the great blessings the Lord had promised for the impending millennial day.

The emotional content of their testimonies had been rekindled through rebaptism, reconfirmation, and sometimes electrifying exhortations.

Now they were in the opening stages of the Utah War. At the very time the Mountain Meadows Massacre occurred, Captain Stewart Van Vliet was three hundred miles north in Salt Lake City, trying to negotiate for supplies for the United States Army which was coming west with a new territorial governor. Van Vliet was told by Governor Brigham Young that the army would not be welcome, would not be supplied, and should not enter Utah. The people of the various settlements were instructed not to sell supplies to the emigrants, as had been their money-making custom in recent years, but to conserve them for the crisis to come. They were also admonished to maintain the good will of the Indians, lest these native Americans join the government forces in opposition.

All of these factors affected the Mormon settlers who confronted the Fancher company.

The historian will also take into account the nature of the emigrants. The Fancher party was a mixture of stable and unstable characters, some of whom were Missourians who apparently did not hesitate to voice their negative opinions of the Mormons. The Fancher party was the first group in 1857 to take the southern route to California. Not meeting the warm welcome they had evidently expected, some of the travelers responded in ways that merely served to provoke the white and red populations of central and southern Utah. The company stopped at Mountain Meadows to let their livestock rest before crossing arid Nevada and southern California. By the time the company arrived in southern Utah, local Indians were eager to run off the emigrants' cattle and do other mischief; the Fancher party was uneasy.

The local Mormons were, of course, watching the course of events, anxious not to become the odd party in a three-sided confrontation. Consultation among secular and religious figures from Cedar City and surrounding communities involved Colonel William H. Dame, the commander of the Nauvoo Legion (the territorial militia), Isaac C. Haight, the stake president, and Bishop Phillip Klingensmith. John D. Lee, the man designated to teach farming to the Indians, was not present in these first discussions.

On Monday, 7 September, the local Paiutes appeared ready to attack the camp, and they wanted their Mormon friends to help them. James Haslam was assigned to ride to Salt Lake City and get Brigham Young's advice. He made the round trip in six days, but by then it was two days too late to implement Young's instructions to let the emigrants pass.

The Indians attacked, inflicting and receiving some casualties. The emigrants then attempted to send out a party to get help from Cedar City. This three-man party was attacked as it tried to get away from the camp and one member was killed. White men were with the Indians when this occurred. Now the question in Cedar City was, "What if the two men who fled back into the camp (and were later killed by Indians as they tried to escape to California) had reported that there were whites as well as Indians besieging the camp?" A critical discussion in which John D. Lee participated concluded that action could not wait. The emigrants must not be permitted to go.

The scheme was carried out the next morning—Friday, 11 September. Lee and two other members of the Nauvoo Legion went into the Fancher camp under a flag of truce and persuaded them to ground their arms and accept an escort into Cedar City. The children were put in a wagon which was led out first. The women and several wounded men were put in a wagon that moved out second. Each of the emigrant men then walked out, unarmed and accompanied by an armed member of the legion. Lee gave the signal and Indians fell upon the second wagon, killing the women and the wounded. Each of the militia men was supposed to shoot the man he was guarding or get out of the way and let the Indians do it. Within a few minutes the deed was done. Only seventeen of the younger children remained, ultimately to be sent back to relatives in Arkansas about a year and a half later.

One of the most revealing episodes in this whole affair is described in Brooks's account: "On the same Sunday morning, September 13, John D. Lee, with a large band of Indians loaded with loot from the massacre, arrived back at Fort Harmony. Entering the gates, they rode around the center of the fort, their tinware jangling and the bundles of clothing tied awkwardly; they rode around once and stopped while the Indians gave their whoop of victory, and Lee declared loudly, 'Thanks be to the Lord God of Israel, who has this day delivered our enemies into our hands'" (p. 139).

This was not the comment of a rabid fanatic, acting alone. John D. Lee was an adopted son of Brigham Young. He had sixteen wives and was a member of the church in good standing. He became, after the event, a branch president in Fort Harmony and served in that capacity for several years.

The Mountain Meadows Massacre was a community mistake, made under stress. It led the participants to take an oath of secrecy that none would ever tell of his or anyone else's part. It was a conspiracy which came to be shared by the larger LDS community as awareness of the event gradually spread.

What followed? In 1859 Klingensmith and Haight were released from their church positions. By then Judge John Cradlebaugh, one of the new federal officials, was trying to get someone prosecuted, it having become common knowledge that the Indians had not acted alone. In 1861 Brigham Young finally visited the site. Apostle Wilford Woodruff recorded his reaction: "We visited the Mountain Meadow Monument put up at the burial place of 120 persons killed by Indians in 1857. The pile of stone was about 12 feet high, but beginning to tumble down. A wooden cross was placed on top with the following words: Vengeance is mine and I will repay saith the Lord. President Young said it should be Vengeance is mine and I have taken a little."[3]

In 1864 John D. Lee was persuaded to resign as branch president, and six years later he and Isaac Haight were excommunicated. Klingensmith disaffected from the church and later became a witness against Lee. In 1874 Haight was reinstated to church membership, while Lee, who had been advised to hide, was at Lonely Dell—now Lee's Ferry—on the Colorado River. Shortly thereafter he came up to southern Utah, was arrested, had two trials, and was executed at Mountain Meadows in 1877.

The first edition of Juanita Brooks's book, as previously noted, was published in 1950. When the second edition appeared twelve years later, it contained this interesting addendum: "For more than a hundred years, the families of John D. Lee have borne the opprobrium of the massacre alone. For that reason, they have welcomed every effort to probe the question; certainly no truth could be worse than the stories to which they were subjected. Now they have special cause to rejoice, for on April 20, 1961, the First Presidency and the Council of Twelve Apostles of the Church of Jesus Christ of Latter-day Saints met in joint council, and: 'It was the action of the Council after considering all the facts available that authorization be given for the reinstatement to membership and former blessings to John D. Lee' " (p. 223).

At least in this instance, setting the historical record straight resulted in righting a historic injustice, because if one of the participants merited excommunication, so did many.

By no means the least disconcerting thing about the de-mythologizing of this tragic affair is the demonstration that initially there was a cover-up. At first no one knew anything. Then as bits and pieces began to be discovered by Judge Cradlebaugh and others who were trying to attach blame to Brigham Young, from an institutional point of view it became a matter of damage control. It is virtually impossible to see what happened to John D. Lee in other terms than that "it is better that one man should perish. . . . " No one but Lee was ever tried. Once he had paid the price, the matter was just dropped. Federal anti-polygamy legislation was entering the enforcement stage, and the menace of polygamic theocracy displaced the massacre as the major concern of federal officials.

Let us turn now to the de-mythologizing of plural marriage.[4]

For a long time after we Mormons abandoned polygamy and decided, in connection with that retreat, to minimize conflict with the world, we played down this aspect of our institutional history. I was a collegian when I learned for the first time that the current president of the church, Heber J. Grant, had been a polygamist. The discovery did not shake my faith, but it did surprise me.

The historical myths prevalent at the time I represented the church in the mission field (1939-41) went something like this:

It is true that at one time 2 to 3 percent of Latter-day Saints practiced polygamy. They practiced it because a surplus of women needed to be provided for in a frontier environment. At the time there was no law against it. When such a law was passed, because Mormons believe in obeying, honoring, and sustaining the law, the practice was discontinued.

From the historian's perspective, that abbreviated version is wrong on *all* counts.

Consider first the extent of plural marriage. Contemporary estimates and some of the best reconstructions based on census and genealogical data suggest that at least 20 percent (and probably more) of the general Mormon population were members of polygamous families — as fathers, mothers, and/or children — at the time and in the areas where plural marriage was practiced. Nels Anderson years ago counted heads in the St. George area; more recently Ben Bennion has made a more sophisticated analysis of census and church records from Dixie and other Utah locations, finding the incidence as high as 50 percent in places.[5] Thus if at least one fourth to one fifth of the total Mormon population was in polygamous family units, then *that* was the extent of plural marriage, not 2–3 percent.

To say next that husbands comprised only about 3 percent of the Mormon polygamous population may not stretch the truth quite so much, but it gives a false impression nonetheless. For if one notes that the incidence of plural marriage increases as one moves up the hierarchy toward the positions at the top, it becomes clear that this was no "fringe" activity. Indeed, participating in "the principle" was virtually a requirement for being a General Authority in the 1860s, 1870s, and 1880s. It was regarded by most participants as obligatory.

Again, if one bears in mind that during the 1880s the church overwhelmingly supported a program of civil disobedience — of defiance or evasion of the laws against plural marriage — the importance of the institution is clear. It was important enough to sacrifice for, important enough to keep Utah from statehood for thirty years after the population was sufficient for admission. There were other considerations, but plural marriage was the most conspicuous and significant single factor which kept Utah out of the Union until 1896.

Consider now the origin of plural marriage. There are questions and problems in broad areas of religion for which documents do not provide answers. Nevertheless, getting into the documents helps to bring people together on the kinds of church-related truth which documents can establish. Historians have established to almost everyone's satisfaction that plural marriage *did* begin with Joseph Smith and was not Brigham Young's invention. In 1982, at a meeting of the John Whitmer Historical Society, the historian of the Reorganized Church of Jesus Christ of Latter Day Saints acknowledged Joseph Smith's initiating role, reversing a position which was for many years a central RLDS tenet.[6] There remains a small controversy about whether Smith may have decided before his death that this doctrinal innovation was so troublesome that it should be abandoned. Some people now take that position, as the founders of the RLDS church did for some years after the death of the prophet.

The origin of plural marriage goes back to the Ohio period, when the concept apparently engaged Joseph Smith's attention in connection with the revising work he was doing on the Old Testament. It was sufficiently discussed to give rise by 1835 to an item which used to be in the Doctrine and Covenants — a statement on marriage denying that Latter-day Saints had anything to do with notions of polygamy. There is persuasive evidence that Joseph Smith took Fanny Alger as his first plural wife in Kirtland about 1835.[7]

In Nauvoo the private teaching began — or was resumed — and marriages were performed in secret in connection with the new doctrines and ordinances associated with the temple. Both teaching and practice began within an inner circle of the prophet's associates before the written revelation now known as Section 132 of the Doctrine and Covenants was read to the Nauvoo high council and a few others in 1843. The document was produced primarily "to convince Emma," who only intermittently came to terms with plural marriage. Linda King Newell and Valeen Tippetts Avery, writing in *Mormon Enigma: Emma Hale Smith* (New York: Doubleday & Co., 1984, pp. 266, 272, 307, 309), suggest that she probably never knew the extent of her husband's involvement in the practice. Later she flatly denied that he had any. By the time her son, Joseph III, came into the leadership of the Reorganized church, he took the same position. Whether that was based on his mother's testimony or a transformation in his own thinking is impossible to determine.

By the time of the prophet's death, a number of leading men and women were in polygamous unions. Many men and women who came to accept this "celestial law" did so after severe struggles. The innovation came not without pain, even as — a half century later — it departed not without pain. Some church leaders rejected the doctrine, and this was one of the factors which led to the *Nauvoo Expositor* and the events at Carthage.

Before the Saints left Nauvoo in 1846, many temple ordinances were performed, many sealings took place, and many polygamous marriages were contracted. At Winter Quarters the practice of plural marriage was more open. By the time the pioneers reached Utah, it was sufficiently public to become an object of remark among non-Mormons passing through. Criticism by non-Mormon judges, journalists, and others prompted the announcement and first public defense of the doctrine and practice in 1852.

The earlier public denials of plural marriage by Joseph Smith and others stemmed, in my view, from the same expedient considerations that led to the Mountain Meadows Massacre cover-up. How else can one account for a man like future LDS church president John Taylor, who had several wives in the Great Basin, saying in France as late as 1850 that the Latter-day Saints did not practice or believe in polygamy? In a proselyting situation, which is essentially a "we-they" situation, one looks for "they" people who are amenable to becoming "we" people. It is a battle against the Devil. One might square his own conscience by reasoning: What we are doing — celestial marriage — is not what the legal prohibitions have in mind or what people mean when they ask about it. If they knew what we know, they would not object to what we are doing. Since they do not, we have to deal with them in terms of their own baser values and understandings.

Let us consider next the "why" question — the arguments advanced to explain and justify plural marriage.[8]

The argument most commonly used in the mythologized, apologetic version is that in a frontier community women need somebody to look after them, and where a surplus of women exists, polygamy is a practical way of doing so. It rests the Mormon commitment to plural marriage on pragmatic social grounds.

This argument was *not* used when polygamy was going on.

It would have been totally irrelevant to the Ohio and Illinois periods of church development, where economic support was not a factor in plural relationships. It was not entirely relevant later on, since in the pioneer west Latter-day Saint women contributed substantially to their own keep. Their husbands were often absent on missions or other church calls, and they looked after themselves and their children, sometimes with help from relatives and church sources. The Victorian image of the dependent wife, helpless without a breadwinner, does not fit most polygamous families — or monogamous families, for that matter — of nineteenth-century Mormonism, so it is not surprising that the social support argument was not used.

When Orson Pratt gave the first full-fledged sermon explaining and justifying the doctrine, he presented themes which were amplified over the years by many LDS writers and speakers. These arguments treated plural marriage as an aspect of celestial, eternal marriage, intended to provide a *worthy* husband for every worthy woman. In this context there *was* a surplus of women in early Mormonism, even though no territorial census ever showed a surplus of females in Utah. In more than one sermon Brigham Young, Heber C. Kimball, and others reproached some of the young priesthood holders for not "squaring their shoulders" and doing their duty by marrying "the daughters of Zion." Then — as now — there were apparently more women worthy of exaltation than partners for them.

A frequently mentioned contemporary justification for plural marriage started with the question which led Joseph Smith to become interested in the first place: Why did Abraham, Isaac, Jacob, and the other patriarchs of the Old Testament have polygamous families if monogamy is the Lord's way? Joseph Smith came to the understanding, as he stated, that these men were blessed because of their righteousness and that the patriarchal order was approved of God anciently and would be part of the restoration.

Some of the theological implications of celestial marriage which were taught and applied in the Nauvoo period were de-emphasized or discontinued later. These included the adopting and sealing of rank-and-file members into the families of leaders of the church, as John D. Lee was sealed to Brigham Young. They also included the sealing of deceased single women to such leaders. Wilford Woodruff's journal details how, on his seventieth birthday, he was accompanied through the new St. George Temple by 154 women, young and old, who received the endowment as proxies for 130 of his deceased wives and twenty-four "near relatives" who were being "added to this list of wives."[9]

As set forth in Section 132 of the Doctrine and Covenants, entry into plural marriage is discretionary, rather than mandatory, for a holder of the Melchizedek Priesthood. If he elects to do so, then assent by his wife, or wives, is obligatory; Emma Smith's particular duty is spelled out in detail. From a privilege initially restricted to those who enjoyed the confidence of the prophet, it soon became, however, an obligation — almost a commandment — for members who were judged worthy to accept it. As outside opposition developed, entering into polygamy or taking additional wives became a way of validating one's testimony or of establishing one's fitness for prominent church offices. As more than one Utah territorial delegate pointed out in arguing against anti-polygamy legislation, the passing of laws would stimulate rather than discourage the practice. There is evidence of upsurges in the number of plural marriages at such times, at least until the mid-1880s.

Consider next the circumstances surrounding the discontinuance of plural marriage. It was a protracted, painful process.

Public opposition to Mormon polygamy began as early as 1835. It continued intermittently and then incessantly, reaching a crescendo in the 1880s. Neither the Woodruff Manifesto prohibiting polygamy nor the statehood of Utah brought it to an end. On the contrary, between 1903 and 1907 there was an extended attempt to prevent Apostle Reed Smoot from being seated in the United States Senate on the grounds that he was a polygamist (which he was not) and that he belonged to an organization which was still secretly encouraging polygamy. When that effort failed, the hue and cry gradually died down, but when I was a missionary a generation later it was still a weapon in the anti-Mormon arsenal.

With regard to the legal status of polygamy, in the states where most of the Mormons lived up to 1847, it would have been perceived as a violation of the law. Ohio and Illinois both had laws against bigamy. When Congress undertook to deal with the subject in 1862, it passed an anti-bigamy act. To the Latter-day Saints there were substantial differences between bigamy and plural marriage, but as they were to discover later, the courts were not prepared to recognize these differences.

In Utah territory the first legal impediment to plural marriage was the Morrill Act of 1862. It was passed by a Republican Congress and signed by President Abraham Lincoln, six years after the first Republican presidential platform called on Congress to prohibit in the territories "those twin relics of barbarism — polygamy and slavery." (For people in our own generation who have come to regard being a Republican as one of the primary attributes of a good Latter-day Saint, it may be humbling to recall that between 1856 and 1896, the Republicans were far more zealous in crusading against our religion than their Democratic counterparts. Many of the Democrats came from the South, where all proposals to reconstruct the customs, lifestyle, and politics of local communities were resisted.)

Once an antipolygamy law was on the books, the position of the Latter-day Saints was that it was unconstitutional, inhibiting that free exercise of religion guaranteed by the First Article of the Bill of

Rights. That position was maintained until 1875, when George Reynolds, President Young's secretary, agreed to be the guinea pig in a test case. (Brigham Young died while the case was in the courts, still convinced in his own mind, I believe, that the Constitution would protect his people in this exercise of their faith.)

In 1879 a unanimous Supreme Court held that the Mormon view was wrong. The judges ruled that the Bill of Rights protects freedom of religious *belief* but not religious practice. One cannot, the court said, use religion as a justification for something that the law could prohibit if it were not done under that cloak. In India, for example, the ritual burning of widows on the funeral pyres of their husbands was commonplace until the British undertook to prohibit it; surely they were right in so doing. Since polygamy was antithetical to nineteenth-century Western civilization, Congress had the right to prohibit it, and the claim of religion did not protect it.

One may speculate on what might have been the fate of the Reynolds case if it had come to the court a hundred years later, but the court, like the court of American public opinion, was then of a single mind. During the next ten or twelve years, the Supreme Court upheld a whole series of measures which Congress and some territorial legislatures adopted to make Mormon polygamists and their church give up this un–American practice. The territory of Idaho went so far as to prohibit all Mormons from voting, with no judicial objection. In 1890 Congress debated a similar measure for Utah; it would bar Latter-day Saints from voting on the ground that they belonged to a conspiratorial organization which was subverting the laws.

Between 1879, when the Supreme Court stripped the Saints of their constitutional defense, and 1890, when the Woodruff Manifesto formally discontinued new plural marriages, what happened? Did it take eleven long years for the court's message to reach Utah and trigger the response mandated by the Eleventh Article of Faith? On the contrary, the position which the church took was one of civil disobedience. Standing with Joshua of old, President John Taylor declared that he and his house would obey the law of God. He went to his grave in 1887 as a fugitive from the law, not having moved from that position. Following his counsel, about 1,300 Latter-day Saints were convicted of unlawful cohabitation or other polygamy-related offenses, and most of them did time in the territorial penitentiary. Some 12,000 Mormon men and women were disfranchised because they were polygamists, and all the Mormon women lost the franchise which they had exercised since 1870.[10]

Almost every LDS family with a pioneer heritage has some cherished tales of "the Underground," where avoidance of the law was an enterprise enlisting the talents — and conspiratorial silence — of young and old. Wilford Woodruff, writing to one of his wives from a hiding place near St. George, advised, "If the marshals come, tell them nothing but the truth, and no more of that than is necessary." People do such things when they confront a crisis of conscience.

The price of civil disobedience was high, and changes in perception and differences in opinion appeared among the Saints as the 1880s took their heavy toll. Some polygamists settled for a fine in exchange for a guilty plea and pledge to obey the law in the future. Others, including members of the church hierarchy, began exploring to see if Utah could somehow achieve statehood and if the government would settle for an end to plural marriages without requiring termination of the relationships already in existence. The territorial judges were saying, without Supreme Court objection, that the only acceptable form of compliance was denying the existence of such bonds. It was not enough to avoid sexual association with the women or even to stop supporting them. Public renunciation was required, at least during the mid-1880s when the judicial crusade was being pursued with greatest fervor.

Under the last of the federal laws, the Edmunds-Tucker Act of 1887, the property of the LDS church was forfeited to the U.S. government to be used for the public schools of the territory, and a dozen other pressures and penalties were brought to bear. Efforts finally reached the critical point in 1890. The president of the church — recording in his diary that he felt, after prayer and inspiration, impelled to act for the preservation of the church — issued the Woodruff Manifesto on 25 September. It announced his intention to comply with the law against plural marrying and counseled the church to follow his example. It is a strangely packaged revelation, hardly an unequivocal commitment to "obey, honor and sustain the law of the land." But it was accepted in the General Conference which followed as binding upon the church, and it was the watershed event insofar as this church-state tug-of-war was concerned.[11]

The actual discontinuance of plural marriage was as painful as the initiation had been. Between 1890 and 1904, when another church president, Joseph F. Smith, issued another manifesto, there was an ambiguous period in which people were not sure how much was being given up and whether the change applied only to Utah or to the United States. Ultimately two apostles were disfellowshipped and one of them was excommunicated for reluctance to surrender on polygamy. A son of John Taylor, Apostle John W. Taylor, was a particularly notable example of that resistance.[12]

I do not know when the last polygamous marriage which was accepted as legitimate by the Mormon leadership took place. After 1904 excommunication was the normal penalty for plural marrying, but there were some exceptions. Plural partnerships continued within the church fold for a half century. The children of such unions are found in prestigious Mormon groups today. They remind us that the reality of LDS plural marriage was far different from the apologetic myth which evolved to divert attention from this distinctive heritage of a people who have preferred in the twentieth century to be noticed for other peculiarities.

This look at two skeletons in the closet of Mormon history reminds us that the past is full of actions which the participants and/or their descendants wish had not happened. If they remain forgotten, they present no problems. If they are rediscovered, how shall we handle them?

It is risky and in the long run counterproductive to substitute myth for historical truth. This is so with personal and family history as well as institutional chronicles. My personal advice to those who confront sensitive information in researching family history is that you do not change *any* of the genealogical information but that you write the personal narrative with your audience in mind. Don't gild the lily but don't spotlight the swamp. The policy I have proposed to families who have commissioned biographies is that I will tell the truth and nothing but the truth but not necessarily the whole truth. This pragmatic formula works best if the difficult facts are peripheral rather than central to understanding the story. Many sponsored biographies have never been published because authors and sponsors differed on how much truth was necessary.

Preserve the documents you find. Think of the loss when Sidney Rigdon's relatives destroyed his 1,500-page biographical manuscript.[13] If you do not want the documents seen now, libraries and archives will gladly keep them where moth and rust cannot corrupt and historians cannot dig until some later time.

Institutions and movements, like the people who comprise them, have a capacity for selectively embellishing, revising, and forgetting aspects of their experience. The myths and half-truths which result are understandable but vulnerable and potentially injurious. However, the exploration of the closets of the historic past, like the investigation of other fields of knowledge referred to in the 88th Section of the Doctrine and Covenants, presents no unmanageable threat to those who agree with Dr. Henry Eyring when he says in *The Faith of a Scientist* (Salt Lake City: Bookcraft, 1969), "In this Church you have only to believe the truth. Find out what the truth is" (p. 43).

— Notes —

1. Brigham H. Roberts, *A Comprehensive History of the Church of Jesus Christ of Latter-day Saints, Century I* (Salt Lake City: Deseret News Press, 1930), 1:441, italics in original.

2. Stephen LeSueur, *The 1838 Mormon War in Missouri* (Columbia: University of Missouri Press, 1987), deals with the context and aftermath of Rigdon's address.

3. Scott G. Kenney, ed., *Wilford Woodruff's Journal*, 9 vols. (Salt Lake City: Signature Books, 1984), 5:577.

4. Mormon plural marriage is generating a body of serious literature, much of it focusing on the beginning and the ending of the practice. A useful survey, with extensive notes and a large but uncritical bibliography, is Richard S. Van Wagoner, *Mormon Polygamy: A History* (Salt Lake City: Signature Books, 1986). My own contributions to the subject are "The Twin Relic: A Study of Mormon Polygamy and the Campaign by the Government of the United States for Its Abolition, 1852-1890," M.A. thesis, Texas Christian University, 1939; "The Mormon Question, 1850-1865: A Study in Politics and Public Opinion," Ph.D. diss., University of California, Berkeley, 1948; "The Political Reconstruction of Utah Territory," *Pacific Historical Review* 27 (May 1958), 2:111-26; and "The Legislative Antipolygamy Campaign," *Brigham Young University Studies* 27 (Fall 1987), 4:109-21.

5. Nels Anderson, *Desert Saints: The Mormon Frontier in Utah* (Chicago: The University of Chicago Press, 1942), 390-419; Lowell "Ben" Bennion, "The Incidence of Mormon Polygamy in 1880: 'Dixie' versus Davis Stake," *Journal of Mormon History* 11 (1984): 27-42.

6. Richard P. Howard, "The Changing RLDS Response to Mormon Polygamy: A Preliminary Analysis," *The John Whitmer Historical Association Journal* 3 (1983): 14–28.

7. Van Wagoner, 1–14, summarizes the research.

8. See David J. Whittaker, "Early Mormon Polygamy Defenses," *Journal of Mormon History* 11 (1984): 43–63; Whittaker, "The Bone in the Throat: Orson Pratt and the Public Announcement of Plural Marriage," *Western Historical Quarterly* 18:3 (July 1987): 293–314.

9. Kenney, 7:329–33.

10. Gustive O. Larson, *The "Americanization" of Utah for Statehood* (San Marino: The Huntington Library, 1971), 91–206, is a good account of the "crusade" years in Utah.

11. See Edward Leo Lyman, *Political Deliverance: The Mormon Quest for Utah Statehood* (Urbana: University of Illinois Press, 1986), for a thorough discussion of this topic.

12. See D. Michael Quinn, "LDS Church Authority and New Plural Marriages, 1890–1904," *Dialogue: A Journal of Mormon Thought* 18 (Spring 1984): 9–105.

13. F. Mark McKiernan, *The Voice of One Crying in the Wilderness: Sidney Rigdon, Religious Reformer, 1793-1876* (Lawrence, KS: Coronado Press, 1971), 171.

9

God's Human Spokesmen

A RECENT EVENT ILLUSTRATES SOME OF THE POINTS I HAVE TRIED to make in preceding essays. Previously, in my exploration of our changing church, I quoted from the October 1984 General Conference address of Elder Ronald E. Poelman, a member of the First Quorum of the Seventy. The language I quoted must have impressed others as well, because it appeared in the *Salt Lake Tribune* and *Deseret News* reports of the conference. It does not appear, however, in the November 1984 *Ensign* magazine, which contains the official proceedings of the conference. What appears instead is a substantially edited version which preserves about 80 percent of the original address, omits about 10 percent, and drastically revises about 10 percent.

Illustrative of the changes are the sentences which begin the talk and the section selected for highlighting in the *Ensign*. I will cite the original language first and then the revision: "Both the gospel of Jesus Christ and the church of Jesus Christ are true and divine. However, there is a distinction between them which is significant, and it is very important that this distinction be understood." Now the revision: "Both the gospel of Jesus Christ and the church of Jesus Christ are true and divine, and there is an essential relationship between them that is significant and very important."

Later in the unedited address is this language: "When we understand the difference between the Gospel and the Church and the appropriate function of each in our daily lives, we are much more likely to do the right things for the right reasons. Institutional discipline is replaced by self-discipline. Supervision is replaced by righteous initiative and a sense of divine accountability." Here is the revision: "When we see the harmony between the Gospel and the Church in our daily lives, we are much more likely to do the right things for the right reasons. We will exercise self-discipline and righteous initiative guided by Church leaders and a sense of divine accountability."[1]

Each of us will of course draw our own conclusions about how and why these changes were made. My understanding is that there is some communication among the General Authorities about the subjects to be addressed in conference but that the talks are not reviewed in advance. Editorial changes are not infrequently made in preparing talks for publication, and sometimes they are rather substantial. I do not know who or what brought about these particular changes or whether this is the first time that changes have been seen as so substantial as to warrant re-recording and re-videotaping an entire General Conference talk.

The points that bear on the tasks of the historian and on the subject at hand seem clear.

1. One of the LDS General Authorities delivered an address that he believed would be helpful to his audience. It was subsequently decided that the address in the form given should not be incorporated in the permanent record. The address was revised by its author, re-video-taped, and re-recorded so that the permanent print and electronic records would be consistent.

2. Historians of the future, perhaps a biographer of Elder Poelman, will either settle for the *Ensign* version without further inquiry or they will find that they have on their hands two versions and a problem.

It is the kind of problem which makes the historian's work so fascinating and frustrating. His task, as I have previously noted, is to recover the past "as it actually happened." He turns to the documents, his primary tools, and finds that all kinds of accidental and deliberate factors affect their reliability as witnesses. He is drawn almost inescapably to the conclusion that historical records are fallible because their authors are human. The makers and preservers of history are unable, or unwilling, to remember the past as it actually occurred. Some of the reasons for this have been explored earlier in these essays.

I come now to the present topic, "God's Human Spokesmen." Because I will focus on the second word in that three-word title, let me clarify first where I stand on the other two words and the concept of prophecy.

1. I believe that God cares about and is accessible to us.

2. I believe that a prophet is a person blessed with special insight to interpret the will of God to humanity.

3. I believe that the test of a prophet is that prescribed by Jesus, "By their fruits ye shall know them."

4. I believe that when Joseph Smith is judged by the many insightful and inspirational passages in his sermons and writings, he satisfies that test.

5. I believe that such teachings as those contained in the sections most recently added to the Doctrine and Covenants show that the prophetic gift remains in the church today.

6. I believe that God will yet reveal many great and important things pertaining to his work.

I turn now to the word "human" in my title and to the *caveat* which has been expressed in preceding essays: I do not believe in the inerrancy of scriptures or the infallibility of prophets. The conviction preceded my professional training, but my work as a Mormon historian has reinforced it.

Here are two authorities, among many, who agree with me.

The first is James Madison, the primary author of the Constitution, a document described in LDS scripture as divinely inspired. He wrote: "When the Almighty himself condescends to address mankind in their own language, his meaning, luminous as it must be, is rendered dim and doubtful by the cloudy medium through which it is communicated."[2] Madison's deism led him to emphasize the communication problem, but his "cloudy medium" recalls the apostle Paul's observation that now we see as "through a glass darkly."

The second authority is the late Elder Bruce R. McConkie: "*Are All Prophetic Utterances True?* Of course they are! This is what the Lord's system of teaching is all about. Anything which his servants say when moved upon by the Holy Ghost is scripture. . . . But every word that a man who is a prophet speaks is not a prophetic utterance. Joseph Smith taught that a prophet is not always a prophet, only when he is acting as such. Men who wear the prophetic mantle are still men; they have their own views; and their understanding of gospel truths is dependent upon the study and inspiration that is theirs. . . . We do not and in our present state of spiritual progression cannot comprehend all things."[3]

The concept of scriptural inerrancy, as this fundamentalist Protestant notion is applied to Mormonism, is that the standard works are verbally inspired. They are more than the Word of God, they are the Words of God. The concept is implicit, though it may not always be intended, in the expression often used by someone reading from the scriptures: "Let's see what the Lord says." It is a comforting idea, reassuring the believer that certain words can be counted on because of where they are found.

From a historian's point of view, several problems make the concept of the verbal infallibility of any writings — even the scriptures — untenable.

The first problem is that *the words themselves were clearly selected and written by men and women.* I include women with a nod to the Song of Deborah in the Old Testament. Their stylistic differences reflect human differences.

The introduction to the fifth volume (pp. xxxiv-xlvi) of Joseph Smith's *History of the Church* (Salt Lake City: Deseret Book Company, 1973) includes a long analysis by its editor, B. H. Roberts, establishing on stylistic grounds that the prophet was the author of the 132nd section of the Doctrine and Covenants. To establish the authenticity of other writings, the church historical department sponsored a study of Smith's writing style. Here are excerpts from Elinore Partridge's paper:

"It may be worthwhile . . . to share some of the insights which I have gained into Joseph Smith, the man, as the result of this stylistic study. In his writings one can see both the spiritual leader giving advice to his people with a definite sense of authority, and the humble, uncertain man needing comfort and reassurance. He shows courage and forebearance [sic], but he also sometimes complains that he is lonely and wishes to hear from family and friends. . . . He mixes eloquent idealism, concerned with spiritual welfare, with homely advice, designed to improve physical welfare, sometimes in the same sentence; for example he tells Emma: 'I am happy to find that you are still in the faith of Christ and at Father Smith's.'

"In examining the writings chronologically, I see little change in Joseph Smith's style from the earliest to the latest manuscripts. However, he becomes increasingly conscious of his calling, as can be seen by the greater authority of his statements and proclamations. Also, his illustrations and examples show increasing sophistication as he broadens his knowledge of history, theology, and nineteenth-century science."

For reasons quite apart from the point under consideration, I like Partridge's last paragraph: "In this close study of Joseph Smith's language, the personal quality which most impressed me was the tremendous sense of joy and vitality. . . . In contrast to the dark visions of Calvinism and the dry, rational theology of Unitarianism, Joseph Smith's pronouncements emphasize the wonder of existence and the love of humanity. Likewise, in contrast to the threats of wrath, judgment, and damnation, which one can find in the statements of some of the early church leaders, there is an undercurrent of understanding and compassion in those of Joseph Smith. Moments of discouragement and anger do occur; however, even at times when he laments the state of mankind, he tempers the observations with trust in God, love for his family, and hope for the future. The love of others, the pleasure in variety, and the joy in living which is apparent in the language of Joseph Smith gives us some real sense, I believe, of what he must have been like as a leader and a friend."[4]

This fits pretty comfortably my image of the man who selected the words with which the revelations communicated through him were made available to our day and age.

In addition to the fact that the words of scripture were selected and written by people, there is clear evidence that *the words have changed* over time. Robert Matthews has analyzed the changes incorporated in the most recent editions of the standard works published by the church. Two illustrations from this comprehensive article will suffice here.

The Book of Mormon phrase "white and delightsome" has become "pure and delightsome." It became "pure and delightsome" in the edition that Joseph Smith revised in 1840, then went back to "white and delightsome" in the next (1852) edition and continued so until 1981. In the meantime, some people even built a little ethno-theology on that language. My purpose here is not to evaluate the two phrases but simply to note that the language has changed — in this instance repeatedly.[5]

Some of us remember when strange names appeared in certain sections of the Doctrine and Covenants, originally used to disguise the names of certain people, places, and concepts. Then the real names were added in parentheses. Now, in the new edition, the strange names are gone, except for a couple whose referents have not yet been identified. One may anticipate that a musty document will one day reveal these two. Then readers of subsequent editions of the Doctrine and Covenants will never know that the strange names were ever there.[6]

Another problem with the notion of verbal inerrancy is that *the words change in meaning and value.* Some of the historic sections of the Doctrine and Covenants are now about as relevant to the church as those sections in Leviticus which Elder Poelman used to illustrate the difference between institutional procedures and eternal principles.

An interesting example of the changing value of words is what has happened to Joseph Smith's inspired revision of the Bible. I was taught years ago that it was not to be used because the prophet had not completed the project. Now it is quoted in the footnotes of the authorized edition of the Bible, used in correlated lessons, treated as a valuable commentary, and in many instances regarded as *the* correct rendition of the scripture.

The change in the status of the Joseph Smith revision has not, however, helped us with another inerrancy problem. Sometimes *the words are inconsistent.* Previously we only had to cope with two biblical versions of the Lord's Prayer, Matthew's and Luke's. Now Joseph Smith's translation has given us a third version, which does not follow either of the other two or the version found in the Book of Mormon (Matt. 6:9-13; Luke 11:1-5; JST Matt. 6:9-15; see also 3 Ne. 13:9-13).

The changes are not radical, but they are not trivial either. What the Savior gave as a model for prayer was presumably stated in a certain verbal formulation, which the writers of scripture subsequently recorded in different languages. If it were translated under divine control—as the dogma of inerrancy requires and our Eighth Article of Faith specifically denies—it ought to come out in a single version. I suspect that one may use any rendition of the Lord's Prayer, including those in other versions than the LDS standard works, and whether it will be heard above the rooftop will be a function of the spirit rather than the words in which the prayer is uttered.[7]

A final problem with scriptural inerrancy is that *some of the words in Holy Writ are incredible.* I will not labor this point because what is incredible for some people is quite credible, even faith-promoting for others. But I did have occasion years ago to ask Elder Joseph Fielding Smith whether we should take the story of Eve's creation literally. He just smiled and said, "Brother Poll, on that subject we need further light." Since that we have received further light. President Spencer W. Kimball stated categorically that this language is to be treated as figurative.[8]

For one who approaches the scriptures as a historian, the prudent course is to seek the most accurate available version of the text, which usually means the one closest to the point of initial utterance or recording. In deciding what to do with the words, the historian is then in the same predicament as other believers, if he chooses to believe. He is likely to take recourse to the same scriptural help which others use — the language of Apostle Paul: "the letter killeth, but the spirit giveth life" (2 Cor. 3:6).

Turning now to prophetic infallibility, I understand this concept to mean that certain individuals, at least in certain circumstances, are absolutely reliable sources of truth. It is not unlike the dogma of papal infallibility in Roman Catholicism, but it is less circumscribed in scope. For Catholics a single individual, the pope, is infallible when he speaks *ex cathedra* in the sphere of faith and morals; such pronouncements are rare.

We Latter-day Saints sustain many men as prophets, seers, and revelators, although we credit the president of the church with more authority than the counselors and other apostles whom we also sustain as prophets. The infallibilitarians among us regard the counsel of these men as absolutely reliable, and their teachings as tantamount to the word of God. With regard to the president of the church, it has been suggested that this power is virtually without limits. This may be a natural by-product of the institutionalization and exaltation of the office of "The Prophet" which has occurred since about 1950.

In a sense it is also a by-product of a popular LDS concept of revelation. Everyone — even little children — may receive absolutely reliable knowledge through the exercise of faith as defined in Moroni 10:4 or D&C 9:8.

One problem with any concept of absolutely reliable individuals or individual statements relates to the quotations read earlier. When is the divine message unaffected by the medium? James Madison answered "never." Elder McConkie suggested that there could be such messages, but he did not specify objective criteria for identifying them.

Let me illustrate, again using musty documents, why historians are inclined to be skeptical of concepts of human infallibility. At the October 1843 conference in Nauvoo, Joseph Smith proposed to drop Sidney Rigdon as his counselor, but the conference refused. The vote was on a motion to sustain Rigdon. It was made by William Marks, whom we can dismiss because he later went wrong, but it was seconded by Hyrum Smith, Joseph's other counselor (HC 6:47-49). Which of the prophet-brothers was inspired?

There were interminable disputes between Brigham Young and Orson Pratt about gospel doctrine. At least twice Young required Pratt to apologize and recant. They disputed, among other things, about two points. Young described Adam as the God of this world, which Pratt disputed. He spoke of God as progressing in knowledge, which Pratt also challenged. If one may judge by current trends in doctrinal interpretation, each of these great gospel witnesses was sometimes right and sometimes wrong. Have the terms "true prophet" and "false prophet" any relevance in evaluating discussions of doctrinal points upon which unambiguous institutional positions have not been defined?[9]

Recently I examined three interesting books — each an edition of Elder McConkie's frequently cited *Mormon Doctrine*. The first came out in 1958 and was withdrawn from circulation after a committee of General Authorities found that it contained many questionable interpretations. The second, which came out in 1966, contains substantial revisions. However, it makes doctrinal statements concerning blacks and the priesthood which were invalidated by a revelation in 1978. The 1979 edition has a revised treatment of that section.[10] I understand that when asked about his earlier statements, Elder McConkie frankly acknowledged, "I was wrong." All of this suggests that *Mormon Doctrine* is a valuable but not infallible commentary. It should certainly be said in fairness to McConkie that he never claimed any edition of the work to be infallibly authoritative, although quite a few Mormons still seem so to regard it.

Wilford Woodruff's multi-volume journal, cited in earlier essays, affords other illustrations of my point. Woodruff is a fascinating individual. He kept an almost daily record for sixty years, and in it he focused on what he heard the prophets say. That he felt was his mission. Early in his career he was one of the scribes who helped write the official church history, and almost until the day of his death he kept a record of what he and his prophet-colleagues did and said. He is an excellent source, even though one encounters in his record many questions, problems, and changes which he lived through without apparent weakening of faith.

Here is what Elder Woodruff wrote on 23 August 1862, after walking on Temple Square with President Young and "Father Morley." They had been talking about speeding construction so that people could take care of their endowments. Young made some not too complimentary remarks about the construction boss and then said, as Woodruff recalled: "If we do not Hurry with this I am afraid we shall not get it up untill we have to go back to Jackson County which I Expet will be in 7 years. I do not want to quite finish this Temple for there will not be any Temple finished untill the One is finished in Jackson County Missouri pointed out by Joseph Smith. *Keep this a secret* to *yourselves* lest some may be discouraged. Some things we should keep to ourselves."[11]

An entire book could be written on the implications of that "musty document." A possible explanation is to insist that Woodruff is not a reliable witness because President Young could not have made such a statement. Given Woodruff's impressive credentials as a diarist, most of us probably find it easier to admit that, at least in this instance, the Mormon Moses was simply wrong.

The human dimensions of our twentieth century prophets are not hard to document. In his office journal, Elder Henry D. Moyle once recorded that he and Elder Harold B. Lee had been stopped outside Las Vegas while driving eighty miles an hour. He noted with just a touch of satisfaction that Lee was driving at the time. (There is some evidence that speeding was an occupational hazard, if not an occupational trait, of the General Authorities in the days when they drove long distances to ecclesiastical assignments.)

The mortal frailties of these prophet leaders go beyond quirky traits and episodic lapses which are likely to provoke chuckles when encountered in the documents. Elder Moyle, for example, had a quick temper, and he took it with him into the Quorum of Twelve Apostles and the First Presidency. It caused him problems. Yet it was closely associated with the dogged determination and self-confidence which made him a mover and shaker. He made a lot of changes, some so profound that a man who is in a position to judge—because he has known them all personally—said to me a few years ago that except for the presidents, nobody in the twentieth century has had as much impact on the church as Henry Moyle. He was a three-dimensional man, capable of inspired insights as to what needed to be done. He was a mediocre preacher; oratory was not his gift. He was smart, and he could be ruthless. He was not a charismatic leader; he was a doer. He was one of God's human spokesmen.

On the issue of prophetic infallibility, I will conclude with an account of what has been for my wife and me the most significant single religious experience in our lives.

A generation ago when I was a fledgling professor, a book appeared which created some stir on the BYU campus: Elder Joseph Fielding Smith's *Man, His Origin and Destiny* (1954). The work takes a dogmatic anti-evolution position on the creation of the earth and man. It gave rise to a public meeting in which I, among others, criticized the book. This in turn resulted in an invitation from the author to visit with him at some convenient time.

My personal connection with Brother Smith was long-standing. He had performed the temple marriage for my father and mother, he had visited in our home in Texas, he had set me apart for the Danish mission when the German missions were closed in 1939, and he had performed the marriage ordinance for my wife Gene and me. It was a friendly relationship. The invitation was not a total surprise, therefore, and Gene and I decided to go in together.

When we arrived at 47 East South Temple a little early on 29 December 1954, it occurred to us to see if President David O. McKay might be available. We had heard from others that McKay was not entirely in agreement with Smith on this matter. As it worked out, President McKay had a little unscheduled time.

So it happened that Gene and I had what must certainly have been, in this century, an uncommon experience for lay members of the church. In back-to-back interviews, with no others present, we were able to spend a half hour with the president of the church, and an hour and a half hour with the man next in line, the president of the Council of the Twelve Apostles.

Here are the notes which Gene and I prepared together within twenty-four hours after returning home:

Notes on a Conversation with President David O. McKay in his Office, 11:00 a.m., Wednesday, December 29, 1954, on the Subject of the Book: Man, His Origin and Destiny. Present: Dr. and Mrs. Richard D. Poll.

Question was raised concerning the obligation of Latter-day Saint teachers in the light of the book's contents.

President McKay said that the book has created a problem. Being written by the President of the Quorum of the Twelve, it has implications which we can appreciate. The book has *not* been approved by the Church; we are authorized to quote him on that. The work represents the opinions of one man on the Scriptures. Brother Smith's views have long been known. Striking the desk for emphasis, President McKay repeated that the book is *not* the authoritative position of the Church. He does not know how it came to be chosen as a text for the seminary and institute teachers last summer, but the choice was unfortunate.

Question was raised concerning the feeling of insecurity felt by many Latter-day Saint teachers.

President McKay said that we have nothing to fear. One man has been earmarked for excommunication, but he is still in the Church and is basically a good man. The President hopes there will be no open clash over the book because of what it would do to the Church as a whole. Nevertheless, we need lose no sleep over this matter, either for the present or the future.

President McKay mentioned Cressy Morrison's *Man Does not Stand Alone* and Le Comte du Nuoy's *Human Destiny* as examples of how scientists have dealt with the problem of man, nature, and God. In his opinion these are two of the outstanding books of this century. We do not know enough of the facts to take a definite position on evolution, but the concept is certainly not incompatible with faith. After all, the process of creation is going on continuously. He and Sister McKay saw it in the eruption of Mount Paricutin in Mexico, and the recent earthquake in Nevada produced one of the most spectacular manifestations of the creative process in recent times.

President McKay concluded by stating that Latter-day Saints accept the Scriptures, but that every man must interpret them for himself. He repeated his advice that we lose no more sleep about this subject.

Two or three times during the conversation President McKay gave the impression that he would like to add something, and then checked himself. Gene and I left with the conviction that he was in complete sympathy with us.

Notes on a Conversation with President Joseph Fielding Smith in his Office, 11:30 a.m. Wednesday, December 19, 1954, on the Subject of the Book: Man, His Origin and Destiny. Present: Dr. and Mrs. Richard D. Poll.

President Smith began by remarking that he wondered if I knew what bad company I was in in the Mormon Seminar [a gathering of Mormon university professors and others]. He described Sterling McMurrin as the leader of the group and a man completely without a testimony. The bishop had planned to institute excommunication proceedings when President McKay had intervened, expressing a desire to talk to McMurrin first. President Smith did not know what the outcome might be.

My defense of the Seminar was based on the fact that many shades of opinion are represented in the group, and that its meetings are not devoted to theological matters but to reports and discussions on topics which are amenable to academic inquiry.

President Smith explained that he had long been concerned over the problem of evolutionist teaching and its effect on testimony, and that he had not published the book entirely on his own initiative. Two or three of the Apostles and two members of the First Council of Seventy had read the manuscript and urged him to publish it. While he did not state that it should be taken as an authoritative Church pronouncement, he declared that he would be happy to retreat from any position taken in the book which could be shown to be contrary to Scripture.

Question was raised concerning whether the Gospel requires a literal acceptance of the Scriptures. President Smith answered in the affirmative. Question was then raised concerning Eve and Adam's rib. President Smith stated that so little information was available on this subject that he did not teach about it. Question was then raised concerning the adequacy of the Scriptural references, about three in all, upon which the doctrine depends that there was no death upon the earth before the fall; this is the doctrine which is chiefly at issue between the literalists and many geologists, biologists, and historians in the Church. His reply was that these Scriptures are unequivocal, and sufficient for him.

President Smith read extensively from the Scriptures to demonstrate that the prophets had taught that the world was created, according to the Lord's time, in seven thousand years; that it has a temporal history of seven thousand years; and that the millennium and the renewing of the earth as a celestial abode are imminent. The recent earthquakes were cited as evidence on this point. He pointed out from Scripture that all life existed spiritually before being placed on the earth, and repeatedly emphasized that God did not create death. Death is the consequence of the Fall, physically as well as spiritually, and for all forms of life as well as the children of Adam. This belief is held to be basic to an understanding of the Atonement of Christ, though President Smith acknowledged that there are those in the Church who apparently accept the Atonement without following the literalist explanation of creation and the Fall.

Asked if there has not been difference of opinion on this subject among the General Authorities since the early days of the Church, President Smith stated that that is possibly true. He is also aware that many prominent scientists of the Church, who have no desire to weaken the faith of members young or old, do not share his views; Henry Eyring had recently spent three hours pointing that out to him without, apparently, giving President Smith opportunity to state his own case.

Agreement was reached that teachers and leaders who seek deliberately to ridicule the Scriptures and undermine confidence in the Church are not entitled to approval or support. Agreement was also reached that scientists can be as dogmatic as other folks, and that scientists who are dogmatically anti-religious are not good scientists.

Questions were raised several times during the conversation about the large number of teachers in the Church who do not denounce or debunk, but who do not find it possible to accept all the doctrines which Brother Smith presents as fundamental. They very much desire to remain tentative in their opinions on these matters. President Smith expressed awareness of the size of the group, and remarked that some of them apparently regard him as without competence in the field of science. He assured that he did not think that they should be excommunicated or barred from teaching.

The conversation concluded with our affirmation that we belong to the group in the Church who finds it difficult to accept all the Scriptures literally, but who are desirous of learning the truth and constructively serving the Church. In the university environment, we are persuaded that the quest for truth flourishes best when the area is rather narrowly defined within which absolute truth is regarded as already known. President Smith approved of the idea, but pointed out that insofar as he is concerned, where the Lord has spoken through the Scriptures, there *is* the truth.

The hour-and-a-half session ended on cordial terms. We left with the impression that President Smith was quite as concerned about justifying his own position as about criticizing ours. Since both sides are apparently on the defensive, we feel more optimistic about the possibility of "peaceful coexistence."

What do we do in this circumstance? Do we go home and pray for a witness as to which of these men whom we have sustained as prophets, seers, and revelators is wrong? Or do we conclude—and this is what we have in fact concluded—that this is a subject on which the mind and will of the Lord is not yet definitively clear to his servants? He created the earth; he knows how he did it. He has not yet seen fit to tell us precisely when and how. This is to me an entirely tenable position—both as a historian and as a believing Latter-day Saint.

In this connection, I found a very helpful formulation in Linda King Newell's and Valeen Tippetts Avery's fine biography of Joseph Smith's first wife, *Mormon Enigma: Emma Hale Smith* (New York: Doubleday, 1984). Noting how many of Joseph Smith's early disciples fell away, they suggest that "those followers who saw Joseph as a *man* with a prophetic calling generally remained faithful, while those who saw him *only* as a prophet and deified him almost invariably found themselves disillusioned" (p. 32).

In distinguishing between whether our prophet leaders are infallible and whether their counsel is dependable, one is not talking about the difference between 100 percent and zero, but between 100 percent and some slightly smaller percentage. It may well be no greater than the old Ivory Soap difference between 100 percent and 99-44/100 percent pure. But the implications of that difference, however small, are profound.

The solution to the problem of fallibility, from the believer's point of view, would seem to be the same with the living oracles as with the scriptures: Learn to live with the human elements which digging in the musty documents, like getting acquainted with the living prophets, will surely disclose. Cherish the pearls of great price which heaven has made available to us through these mortal channels.

— *Notes* —

1. The excerpts are from an audiotape of the General Conference broadcast, 7 Oct. 1984, and from the *Ensign* 14 (Nov. 1984), 11:64-65.

2. Quoted in Alpheus T. Mason, "Free Government's Balance Wheel," *Wilson Quarterly*, Spring 1977, 97.

3. Letter to "Honest Truth Seekers," 1 July 1980, 4, copy in my possession.

4. Elinore H. Partridge, "Characteristics of Joseph Smith's Style and Notes on the Authorship of the Lectures on Faith," Task Papers in LDS History, No. 14, Dec. 1976, 19-20.

5. Robert J. Matthews, "The New Publications of the Standard Works — 1979, 1981," *Brigham Young University Studies* 22 (Fall 1982), 4:398-99.

6. Ibid., 406, 408. The relevant D&C sections are 78, 82, 92, 96, 103, 104, and 105. A recent non-scriptural illustration of names disappearing down Orwell's "memory hole" is the omission in the *Deseret News 1987 Church Almanac* of the names of former church patriarchs; previous editions included them in the biographical sketches of past and present General Authorities. This listing was restored in the 1989-90 almanac.

7. The current church reliance on the King James version of the Bible, like the endorsement of King James English as the language of prayer and the aversion to ritual candles, almost certainly owes more to President J. Reuben Clark's scholarly preferences and his idiosyncratic views of appropriate worship than to LDS scriptures or doctrine.

8. Spencer W. Kimball, "Privileges and Responsibilities of Sisters," *Ensign* 19 (Nov. 1979), 11:71.

9. Gary James Bergera, "The Orson Pratt-Brigham Young Controversies: Conflict within the Quorums, 1853 to 1868," *Dialogue: A Journal of Mormon Thought* 13 (Summer 1980), 2:7-58.

10. Bruce R. McConkie, *Mormon Doctrine* (Salt Lake City: Bookcraft, 1958), 129-31, 548; ibid. (1966), 527, 610; ibid. (1979), 526-28. Other evidence that Elder McConkie's explanations of certain gospel-related subjects changed over the years may be found in these volumes.

11. Scott G. Kenney, ed., *Wilford Woodruff's Journal*, 9 vols. (Salt Lake City: Signature Books, 1984), 6:71.

IO

The Challenge of
Living with Change

WE ALL LIVE WITH CHANGE, WHETHER WE REGARD IT AS A PLIGHT
or an opportunity. We live with change, not merely because the world
is always changing but because our understanding of that world is
also changing. No happy valley is impervious to new insights and
information — and their challenges.

The foregoing essays reflect more than fifty years of living
with history — with the records and the processes of change. The observations and conclusions that follow are partly professional, partly personal. They address two questions: What have I learned from the study
of Mormon history? and How have my studies affected my faith as a
Latter-day Saint?

My answer to the first question — and I am only one of many
historians who are both Mormons and students of Mormon history —
combines and augments conclusions suggested in the previous essays:

1. The historian's goal — to recapture the past "as it actually
happened" — is for many reasons unattainable.

2. Institutions and movements, like the people who comprise
them, have a capacity for selectively embellishing, revising, and forgetting aspects of their experience.

3. The creation of historical myths — idealized versions of
important past experiences — is an inevitable process which contributes to the pursuit of righteousness to the extent that it provides role
models and motivating traditions which are consistent with truth.

123

4. Historians, with their documents, contribute to the pursuit of righteousness when they check the myth-making capability to generate and perpetuate untruth and half-truth and to sanctify unrighteousness.

5. The historian who looks at church history finds confirmation of the distinction between unchanging gospel principles, which are accessible through the eye of faith, and changing institutions, which may be studied through documents and other tools of the historian's craft.

6. Given what history (and other disciplines) tell us about institutional dynamics, the current vigor of the Mormon church is *prima facie* evidence that it has changed since 1830.

7. In the perspective of the Ninth Article of Faith, past changes in the LDS church should not surprise us nor should the virtual certainty of future changes distress us.

8. At this point in the development of each, Utah and the Mormons are what they are because their lives have been so intertwined; the association has been a symbiotic relationship in the mutually interactive sense.

9. As to the future of the symbiosis, it is much more likely that the Mormons will continue to influence the development of the state than that Utah will continue to influence Mormonism as Salt Lake City becomes the center of an international church.

10. Part of our changing past is our changing perception of our heroes as new documents and new insights force us to take fresh looks at the mythic figures they have become.

11. The process of historical inquiry, which constantly alters and expands our understanding of George Washington and Abraham Lincoln, Abigail Adams and Eleanor Roosevelt, may be expected to continue to affect our understanding of the heroic figures of Mormonism.

12. Historical inquiry provides little support for doctrines of infallibility and inerrancy, whether applied to historic documents, persons, or institutions.

13. The exploration of the historic past, like the investigation of other fields of knowledge, presents no unmanageable risks to those who accept Henry Eyring's challenge: "In this Church you have only to believe the truth. Find out what the truth is" (*Faith of a Scientist* [Salt Lake City: Bookcraft, 1969], 41).

The central problem in following the Eyring recommendation is what learning theory calls "cognitive dissonance." We learn things which do not fit with what we have learned before, and the experience can be jarring. It may be a little jar or it may be traumatic. Trauma is likely to occur when new information is inconsistent, incongruent, or incompatible with what we have previously regarded as *important* truth.

For example, emerging modern European society had difficulty when somebody suggested, on the basis of new data, that the earth is not the center of the universe. Many important concepts and values hung on pre-Copernican perceptions of heaven and earth. People had a hard time adjusting to the new knowledge; indeed, a few people in our own day still resist.

Our discussion of myths and documents presented several examples of cognitive dissonance, most of which generated little or no stress. Some myths do have a trauma potential; when I told the following story to a Sunstone Theological Symposium audience, an academic colleague suggested that I might be unintentionally undermining people's faith in President Hugh B. Brown.

Before turning to the story, I remind you that the historical accuracy of a faith-promoting story is not relevant to its value unless one makes that depend on its factual correctness. Infallibilitarians and literalists can create problems for other believers, and sometimes for themselves, by insisting that basic components of faith are inseparably connected with sharply delineated historic contexts.

"The Case of the Disappointed Canadian Officer" concerns one of the favorite LDS General Authorities of the twentieth century. One of the great experiences of my life was working with my good friend, the late Eugene Campbell, on a biography of Hugh B. Brown. Our last meeting with President Brown was to report that the book was in press. He was bedfast and near death, but he still had his smile and his wit. When we told him the book was almost ready, he said, "We can call it my obituary." I protested, "Oh no, President Brown. This is far more than that." He said, "Maybe we should call it 'Son of Obituary.'"

Many Mormons have heard the story of Hugh Brown and the currant bush. In summary, it tells how Brown, as an officer in the Canadian Army in World War I, took a contingent of troops to

England, expecting to lead them into combat and anticipating a promotion in rank. At a critical point he was called in for an interview. His superior officer, a general, fussed and stalled and then was called away, giving Brown opportunity to glance at the papers on the desk. On his service record, in very legible letters, was written, "This man is a Mormon." Denied the appointment, Major Brown was inclined to be resentful. Then he recalled the currant bush complaining of being pruned too short, and his response: "You've been cut back so that you can get the growth that you're intended for."

It is a wonderful story. The problem with it is that, on the basis of the documents as I read them, it is not quite true. Hugh B. Brown *was* a good and very popular officer, and he *did* go overseas expecting advancement. But when he got to England, he discovered what the history of that war clearly establishes — that more enlisted men than field grade officers were being killed in France. By 1917 recruits were going to the front as replacements, not as new combat units, and there was no place for all of the officers who had trained them. The journal of Major Brown's aide suggests that personal favoritism *was* behind the selection of one of the other contenders for advancement; it also reports, however, that Brown was never granted the interview he requested. He returned to Canada, and as the soldiers he took over began to die, some Albertans made snide comments about "slackers." He wrote in his journal then: "I spent most of . . . May at home visiting family and friends and learned by bitter experience of being misjudged, for some who had appeared to be my friends were most harsh in their criticism of my returning home, thinking I came on account of my fear of the battle line. But God knows I did not have any choosing and that I tried to do my duty and play the game."[1]

In such circumstances, one can imagine the parable of the currant bush beginning to take shape. From the time it first appeared in print in 1939 until President Brown's death thirty-six years later, it evolved further, as such tales do. President Brown was a story teller *par excellence*, and he knew what good story tellers know — that you use what works with the crowd. It may be that he came in time to believe the mythologized version of the event, in which case there would have been no conscious dishonesty in telling it. Who has not discovered the capacity of his own memory to remodel the past?

What is one to do with this story? Gene Campbell and I never had a chance to ask President Brown about it, so we fretted, then told the World War I events as we had reconstructed them and fell back on Elder Harold B. Lee for protection. In writing of President Brown's appointment as an assistant to the Quorum of Twelve Apostles, Lee had mentioned the military disappointment in terms that we felt the documents supported, so we quoted him.[2] We never really made a judgment on the currant bush story but used it in another chapter without the details.

What to do with a story in a book is a small thing. What separating the myth from the documents does to the image of President Hugh B. Brown, or any other religious or secular leader, each individual must experience for him- or herself. I still love and respect President Brown very much after finding what I believe is a small chink in his armor.

We should be very cautious about passing judgment on those who create historical myths. Henry D. Moyle used to scold missionaries when they asked to have their missions cut short, mentioning his own two-and-a-half years of service in Germany. His own journal records that when he had been twenty-three months on his mission he was permitted to enroll in the University of Freiberg with the understanding that he would help the missionaries there while he was in school. The last seven months of his mission were spent as a student at Freiberg, where the East German temple now stands. The point he stressed with the missionaries a generation later was a good one — good enough to alter his memory or appease his conscience.

A myth does not go anywhere unless it meets needs. (The same may be said for folklore, which is another way people distill out of experience that which is of value. Even a community as young, with members as sophisticated, as the Mormons has its treasury of folklore.)

I turn now to a case of more traumatic dissonance — a case in which the discovery of documents has had substantial impact upon an important faith-related historical myth. It also illustrates several approaches to dissonance management and permits me to draw some conclusions. It is "The Case of the Book of Abraham."

The rediscovery of some of the Egyptian papyri associated with The Pearl of Great Price certainly challenged the LDS tradition — the historical myth — that the Book of Abraham is a literal translation of an ancient document. The recovery and identification of the *sn-sn* text presents a two-fold problem of dissonance.

One problem involves the LDS concept, or concepts, of translation. If the book did not derive in any linguistic sense from the papyrus documents with which its origin is associated, was there a significant connection between them?

The second problem involves the LDS concept, or concepts, of revelation. If the book did not come from the papyri, did it come from God?

The dissonance — the incongruity — between the pictures and text of the Book of Abraham bothered me when I read the work as an undergraduate, possibly because of my exposure to textual criticism at Texas Christian University. Being under no urgent necessity to impose harmony, I adopted stimulating and helpful ideas from the book and left the questions alone — as any lazy Liahona would. When the recovery of the papyri forced the issue, I sampled a little of the apologetic literature, found it unsatisfactory, and left my own position unarticulated until James B. Allen and Glen M. Leonard offered a superbly phrased formulation in *The Story of the Latter-day Saints* (Salt Lake City: Deseret Book, 1976): "The exact relationship between the ancient scrolls and the printed text of the Book of Abraham has been a matter of controversy. . . . Although translations by both LDS and other scholars made it clear that [the papyri] were not part of the Abraham text, Church scholars . . . suggested that the scrolls themselves may simply have been the catalyst that turned Joseph's mind back to ancient Egypt and opened it to revelation on the experiences of Abraham. . . . Joseph may have received these ideas the same way he did those of the inspired translation of the Bible. In that instance, acting without original documents, the Prophet's only claim was that by divine inspiration he was able to replace incorrect with correct ideas and restore the original biblical meaning. . . . Even the Book of Mormon was translated by the gift and power of God rather than through any prior knowledge of ancient language. When applied by Mormons to Joseph Smith, the term 'translator' thus has a special meaning" (p. 68).

Why Joseph Smith thought it important to provide partial explanations of the pictures associated with the Book of Abraham is, to me, part of the larger enigma that is the prophet. I wish that the

Allen-Leonard concept of "translator" had wider currency among today's Latter-day Saints.

This brings me to the second problem: If the Book of Abraham is not from the papyri, is it from God?

The Allen-Leonard formulation implies an affirmative answer, to which I will add this personal observation: If one prophet can hear God in a burning bush, is it not also possible for another to be inspired by an ancient burial text?

This was less of a problem during my undergraduate days, because there was less pressure within the church to identify revelation with such dogmas as prophetic infallibility and scriptural inerrancy. We quoted the Eighth and Ninth Articles of Faith as though the words "as far as it is translated correctly" and "He will yet reveal many great and important things" had real meaning. We took Joseph Smith seriously when he said that some of his own revelations might be from man or the devil, and it helped us to cherish the great insights in his teachings without worrying unduly about Zelph or the Kinderhook plates or whether that figure in the Pearl of Great Price is really Abraham on an altar.

The relatively recent preoccupation with institutional unity and individual security has brought us today, however, to the point where it appears that dissonance must be denied. This effort to make everything tidy does not, in my view, stem from doctrine or even institutional necessity but from the idiosyncracies of some leaders and the psychological needs of many followers. Without digging further into the "why" question, I want to make a point or two about the prevalence of the denial of dissonance and the degree of its success.

Authoritarian pronouncement is, of course, one technique of denial, well represented in the literature of the new LDS orthodoxy. *Since* the gospel is true and all truth is harmonious, perceived incongruities in church teaching and practice must reflect the frailty of the perceiver. *Since* the scriptures are substantially inerrant, now that the footnotes from the prophet's revision are there to smooth out rough places in the Bible, neither fossils nor floating axes need trouble the faithful. *Since* the public utterances of the prophets are almost always inspired and cover almost every consequential topic, one needs only quasi-authoritative help with the odd incongruity in the *Journal of Discourses* to remain secure against the buffetings of dissonance and doubt.

Reliance on selected "experts" is another way to finesse dissonance. My good friend Hugh Nibley is a superb example. Since he gained unique status as "defender of the faith" with his rebuttal to Fawn M. Brodie's biography of Joseph Smith, *No Man Knows My History*, he has become a security blanket for Latter-day Saints to whom dissonance is intolerable. Dr. Nibley's contribution to dissonance management is not so much *what* he has written as *that* he has written. On the basis of no scientific evidence, I suggest that relatively few Latter-day Saints read the Nibley books that they give to one another or the copiously annotated articles he has contributed to church publications. It is enough for most of us that they are *there*. We have a scholar who has met the scholars on their own ground and established that the dissonances they point to are only apparent, not real. As Hugh Nibley retires from the lists, other defenders of the faith are coming forward to perform this service.

Discouraging inquiry is yet another way of denying dissonance. I refer not only to the formal and informal restraints on academic investigation with which recent LDS history is spotted but to the general inhibition of free discussion in the educational programs of the church. As a teacher who sees questions as stepping stones to learning in both college and church classes, I am perturbed that the highly structured and correlated lessons prepared for our Sunday and seminary consideration repress inquiry, even by the teachers, and treat questions from class members as impediments to "covering the material." Where the scriptural segments under study have the potential to raise questions, teachers are counseled to use pre-packaged answers and avoid "controversy." The apparent intent and observable result is to produce bland instruction in which acquiescent students read or recite on cue and even contradictory opinions are heard without demurrer. The capacity to perceive dissonance is dulled.

There is a touch of irony in all this, because Mormons of both Iron Rod and Liahona complexion have shown remarkable capacity to accommodate dissonance when it has been unavoidable. The Pearl of Great Price has survived the recovery of the papyri, with Dr. Nibley's help or in spite of it. The discovery that certain of God's children are not going to have to wait until the Millennium for the priesthood has been accommodated with grace even by those whose prior concepts of the plan of salvation were shaken by it. The Joseph Smith III blessing document had already been accommodated by most testimonies before it was exposed as a forgery, requiring no accommodation. As seerstones and freemasonry are demonstrated to have figured prominently in the Restoration, similar outcomes may be expected.

What is the moral? A cynical view might be that belief will overcome evidence. I prefer a more hopeful, helpful interpretation. Given our human limitations and the cautions expressed in the Eighth and Ninth Articles of Faith, we must expect to encounter cognitive dissonance, even in the sphere of faith. As God's free agent children, we have the right and responsibility to choose how we will cope with it.

So how has the study of our changing past affected the faith and commitments of this Mormon historian?

The study of history in general, and church history in particular, is faith testing. It will, in my view, almost certainly weaken faith if faith is defined as certitude. It may strengthen faith if faith is defined as commitment. Certitude is a state of mind; commitment is a state of living.

For almost half a century I have been teaching history, mostly American, and studying history, mostly Mormon. I have been sustained in this enterprise by the sheer pleasure of living with the past, by the stimulation of professional relations, and by the prophetic assurance that this is an honorable vocation. Does not the voice of revelation urge us to become more perfectly informed of "things which have been, things which are, things which must shortly come to pass; things which are at home, things which are abroad; the wars and perplexities of nations, and the judgments which are on the land" (D&C 88:79)?

Most historians of Mormonism, whether Mormon or Gentile, define their mission in purely professional terms. They examine the documents and other records and report their findings, quite aware of two humbling considerations: Their best efforts cannot recapture the past "as it actually happened," for reasons discussed earlier in these essays; and not more than a twentieth or a fiftieth of today's Latter-day Saints are interested in their writings. Still, they are available for those who encounter questions or who are interested in pursuing the history of their faith. This motivated church historian Leonard Arrington and his associates during what had been described as "the

Camelot years" in the church's historical department, and it motivates almost all scholars writing Mormon history today.

Because some people seem to feel that historical study is inherently destructive of religious faith, I wish to report that some of the finest spiritual experiences of my life have been the devotionals at the annual meetings of the Mormon History Association. At a worship service in the Kirtland Temple, arranged jointly by representatives of the RLDS and LDS churches, we sang to the accompaniment of a brass choir, "The Spirit of God Like a Fire is Burning." It was a particularly moving experience because almost every singer knew some of the history of that sacred place. Meetings in the Sacred Grove, the chapel at Graceland College, the Assembly Hall in Salt Lake City, and the RLDS Auditorium in Independence, Missouri, were all inspirational. The stories of Haun's Mill, Benbow Farm, the Red Brick Store, the Mountain Meadows tragedy, the Ribble River baptisms, and Winter Quarters had special impact when told on site by men and women who had studied them. The notion that religious truth cannot stand exposure to the past has only to be stated to be dismissed.

Mormon historians would not wrestle so much with this problem of "faithful history" if they were not, in fact, so concerned about it. What is the "faithful" treatment of a document? If Joseph Smith actually wrote a letter, then what that letter says has to be dealt with. If you are dealing with Joseph Smith as a whole person, then you cannot just ignore it because it has incorrect spelling or contains some ideas that have not stood the test. You fit it in; you accept it like a lot of other things that do not fit in neatly.

I have found that history gives more information than answers. It is a better tool for identifying error than for validating truth; it gives one more certainty about what was not and is not than about what is or may be.

This leaves ample room for faith and for differences of opinion on how faith and history relate. A didactic view has been expressed by a prominent critic of some LDS historiography. "Some things that are true," he points out, "are not very useful." A pitfall to be avoided, he cautions, is the "temptation for the writer or the teacher of church history to want to tell everything, whether it is worthy or faith promoting or not."[3]

My professional and personal view of "faithful history" embraces these propositions:

The scriptural counsel to give milk before meat (Heb. 5:11-15) recognizes that seekers after truth do not all start at the same place, proceed at the same pace, or have the same intellectual needs or goals; it does not, however, endorse a universal diet of milk only.

No one — not even children and prospective converts — should be wittingly taught falsehoods about the past.

All Saints should be taught, as soon as they can comprehend the idea, that God works through fallible men and women, and that these frailities are sometimes revealed in surprising and distressing ways.

Historical truth, like other facets of truth, should be rigorously pursued, untrammeled by institutional restraints, so that it is available to Saints and Gentiles who are curious about the past.

Historical findings should be shared with sensitivity and love, not in the spirit of the debunker or sectarian crusader.

Historical knowledge should be promulgated humbly, because it is almost certainly not "the whole truth and nothing but the truth."

Which brings me back to the point earlier made about history being a better tool for identifying error than for validating truth. This is why I can say that the study of history has not weakened my faith but changed it. I do not now believe some of the historical propositions that were once part of my testimony. I am a Liahona Mormon with even fewer firm answers than I had as a youth. But as I once wrote in "What the Church Means to People Like Me," I find in the gospel — as I understand it now — "answers to enough important questions so that I can function purposefully without answers to the rest."

To me the gospel means that the history of humanity is not already written, not even for the Lord himself. What we are presently engaged in is not a drama without a point or a fortuitous comedy of errors or a foredoomed tragedy or a fully scripted pageant in which we are all mimes. God is the producer and Jesus Christ is the central actor in the play, but what happens on the stage depends significantly upon the choices of all members of the cast.

The study of the past helps all of us — not just "people like me" — to make wise choices. It is thus profitable in spite of the fact that it rocks the ark of faith. I agree with those who have pointed out that the efficacy of the gospel does not depend on beliefs about the past, which may become unbelievable. I know that the inspirational power of the scriptures does not depend on God's having written every word. I see the church as a human institution permeated with a sense of divine calling, changing over time in response to new perceptions of God's will. I work — most of the time happily — at being a good Mormon because *these* things are important to me: the fellowship of the Saints; the good counsel that prophet- leaders almost always give; the inspiration and insight to be found in sacred scriptures; the rituals, customs, and ordinances that remind me that history *is* going somewhere; the consolation of prayer; the challenges to service; and the reinforcement of that "hope in Christ" which gives meaning to all life.

I confront the golden years — and the years beyond — with optimism and gratitude.

Notes

1. Eugene E. Campbell and Richard D. Poll, *Hugh B. Brown: His Life and Thought* (Salt Lake City: Bookcraft, 1975), 70.

2. Ibid., 68.

3. Boyd K. Packer, *The Mantle is Far, Far Greater than the Intellect* (Salt Lake City: The Church of Jesus Christ of Latter-day Saints, 1981), 4.